## Praise for *Questioning for Formative Feedback*

Imagine being in lessons dominated by questions that require less than three-word responses. Imagine spending the day in a class and no one listens to you. Imagine receiving feedback that proves you were not understood. Not in Jackie Walsh's class—where questions cause thinking, give feedback to the teacher about their impact, lead to wonder, elicit student thinking, initiate and sustain feedback conversations, and help determine next steps in teaching and learning. Questions start—not finish—dialogue, engage (not exclude), lead to uptake, and are invitations to maintain learning. This is the essence of *Questioning for Formative Feedback*.

—John Hattie
Emeritus laureate professor, Melbourne Graduate School of Education
Chair, Board of the Australian Institute for Teaching and School Leadership

Walsh is a master of the art of questioning. In this new book, she raises the bar even higher by linking quality questions to the thinking, dialogue, and feedback that can result in learning. Importantly, she ensures that questioning for formative assessment is *informative*. The strength of this book lies in its links between principles and practice. I can't wait to apply these ideas to my own practices.

—Nancy Frey
San Diego State University, Department of Educational Leadership

Leave it to Jackie Walsh, leading expert in the principles and practices of quality questioning, to frame her latest work, *Questioning for Formative Feedback*, with a powerful question: How can we harness three powerful processes—formative feedback, quality questioning, and purposeful dialogue—to optimize student learning? Grounded in decades of research and practice, Walsh has uncovered the synergy among these three potent accelerators of student achievement, motivation, and engagement and provided us with a practical guide for realizing their promise in the classroom. Although I've been a student of formative assessment for many years, I will never again be able to think of it as separate from student inquiry, agency, and discourse. Walsh's fresh perspective has left me both inspired by a vision of classrooms alive with authenticity and excitement and eager to put her practical tools to work.

—Nancy Love
Senior consultant, Research for Better Teaching
Author of *The Data Coach's Guide for Improving Learning for All Students*

Dr. Walsh has done it again. *Questioning for Formative Feedback* will be our go-to resource for using quality questions for formative feedback. I believe that grading is fading into feedback, and our teachers need the tools and resources to make this happen in our classrooms with our students. To put it simply, Dr. Walsh offers practical tools and ideas that work. At Oxford High School, we saw growth in our ACT data during a pandemic. This was no accident. Our work with Dr. Walsh and our commitment to quality questioning is the reason we were able to achieve this success. I highly recommend this book to all educators who are committed to partnering with their students to enhance classroom dialogue, formative feedback, and student learning.

—Heath M. Harmon
Principal, Oxford High School, Oxford, Alabama

I have been a believer in the power of quality questioning since my introduction to it several years ago. As an instructional leader on an elementary campus, I know that time is of the essence and with so many competing interests in the classroom, the use of questioning and an expectation of authentic student engagement in thinking is the essential tool to achieve high levels of learning for all. This book seeks to propel us forward from the antiquated notion that numerical grades are feedback on student learning to a space where teachers are designers of rich learning experiences that inspire students to seek true feedback for their own learning and define their next steps.

—Deanna Dolford Jackson
Principal, Watts Elementary School, Cibolo, Texas

While most educators agree that giving students a voice in their own education and designing learning with the students in mind are sound and meaningful practices, many educators struggle to bring this approach to fruition. Understanding the importance of quality questioning, purposeful dialogue, and formative feedback is important; being able to transfer this understanding into classrooms with students is a critical challenge for educators. Dr. Walsh provides an easy-to-understand, familiar GPS voice to help us make this transfer of principles into actual daily classroom practice. This book builds on a lifetime of work and is truly a manual for educators looking to increase student achievement for today's generation of learners. Not only does Dr. Walsh provide a step-by-step approach for applying the research and learning behind quality questioning, purposeful dialogue, and formative feedback, but she also addresses the importance of meshing these practices with social and emotional needs in order to help students be curious, motivated, self-regulated learners—something we all should work for in our classrooms each day.

—Stoney M. Beavers
Assistant director, Alabama Best Practices Center

Jackie Walsh's *Questioning for Formative Feedback* is a must-read for everyone involved in teacher preparation. Her book provides a framework for understanding questioning, dialogue, and formative feedback for emerging candidates through career educators. The blueprints, tools, protocols, and artifacts included in the book provide approaches that are important for preservice candidates' ability to understand the value of questioning for students and teachers. She provides examples that allow preservice candidates to see roles and responsibilities for all involved in the classroom community engaged in effective questioning practices.

—Karen Granger
Assistant professor, UNC Pembroke
Regional director, NC New Teacher Support Program

The essential question Jackie Walsh has pursued throughout her influential career is succinctly stated in her introduction to this essential new book: *How can we infuse school learning with the authenticity and excitement associated with real-life experiences?* Her answers—offered in clear, practical, actionable language honed in a series of influential works over several decades—come down to this: *The strategic use of quality questioning, purposeful dialogue, and formative feedback.* Readers of this succinct, illuminating guide to formative practice will learn how to become strategic users of these powerful tools. Today's teachers are hungry to help students gain ownership of learning. Here's how.

—John Croft Norton
Founder and coeditor, MiddleWeb.com

What an incredible gift Jackie Walsh has given to preservice teachers with her new text, *Questioning for Formative Feedback*. Through careful explanations of questioning, formative feedback, and dialogue—along with extensive classroom artifacts, videos, and questioning protocols—Dr. Walsh supports new teachers with a firm foundation of being both a lesson designer and learning facilitator in any subject area. Lifting student achievement is paramount in our post-pandemic efforts. This text serves as a blueprint for young teachers who are learning to craft supportive, solid structures in their teaching environments while working to increase student achievement. As a former district administrator, I believe veteran teachers who study and implement this text will refine their current practices of questioning and feedback and, ultimately, increase their capacity to affect student learning. Questioning and formative feedback cause students to think more deeply about the work they are doing and move them toward better learning outcomes. Additionally, as higher-education instructors work to support student interns, the questioning protocols and formative feedback routines Dr. Walsh provides in the text will support them as reflection experiences will be strengthened. I am ready to place this text in the hands of both new and veteran teachers as well as higher-education faculty. It will be exciting to watch the positive impact this text guarantees as teachers employ great questioning, offer formative feedback, and create frequent dialogue around any topic.

—Paige Raney
Chair, Division of Education, Spring Hill College, Mobile, Alabama

Jackie Walsh's masterful ability to harness the power of quality questioning and its use in K–12 classrooms is on full display in *Questioning for Formative Feedback*. She demonstrates how the notion of good, thoughtful questioning can allow student-teacher interaction to flow from thinking to dialogue to feedback, raising student learning to high levels. Through real-life scenarios and useful protocols, classroom leaders will find support for developing and designing formative frameworks for student experiences throughout this amazing book. It is a must for teachers focusing on high levels of learning for all students.

—Bill Kennedy
Director (retired), Principal Leadership Academy
Hamilton County (TN) Schools/Public Education Foundation,
Chattanooga, Tennessee

As a teacher, I know how challenging and important cognitive engagement is to student learning. *Questioning for Formative Feedback* offers practitioners a much-needed resource to develop student ownership for their thinking and learning. In this book, Jackie Walsh balances theory with practice, providing the reader with a sound rationale for intentional use of quality questioning and dialogue to produce feedback that unlocks student learning. More importantly, she illustrates practical ways for teachers to make these connections for themselves and their students. The tools provided in charts and graphical format will be of immeasurable use to me and all teachers who read this book.

—Brad R. Waguespack
Environmental science teacher, Vestavia Hills High School,
Vestavia Hills, Alabama

Questioning for Formative Feedback

Many ASCD members received this book
as a member benefit upon its initial release.
Learn more at **www.ascd.org/memberbooks**.

• • • • •

**Other ASCD publications by Jackie Acree Walsh:**

*Generating Formative Feedback*
(Quick Reference Guide)

―――――――

*Improving Classroom Discussion*
(Quick Reference Guide)

―――――――

*Questioning for Classroom Discussion: Purposeful
Speaking, Engaged Listening, Deep Thinking*
with Beth Dankert Sattes

―――――――

*Questioning Strategies to Activate Student Thinking*
(Quick Reference Guide)

# Questioning for Formative Feedback

## Feedback

### Meaningful Dialogue to Improve Learning

## Jackie Acree Walsh

ascd

Alexandria, VA USA

**a ascd**

1703 N. Beauregard St. • Alexandria, VA 22311-1714 USA
Phone: 800-933-2723 or 703-578-9600 • Fax: 703-575-5400
Website: www.ascd.org • Email: member@ascd.org
Author guidelines: www.ascd.org/write

Ranjit Sidhu, *CEO & Executive Director;* Penny Reinart, *Chief Impact Officer;* Genny Ostertag, *Managing Director, Acquisitions & Editing;* Allison Scott, *Senior Acquisitions Editor;* Julie Houtz, *Director, Book Editing;* Jamie Greene, *Editor;* Thomas Lytle, *Creative Director;* Donald Ely, *Art Director;* Samantha Wood, *Graphic Designer;* Kelly Marshall, *Production Manager;* Christopher Logan, *Senior Production Specialist;* Valerie Younkin, *Senior Production Designer;* Shajuan Martin, *E-Publishing Specialist*

PAPERBACK ISBN: 978-1-4166-3116-3   ASCD product #119006

PDF EBOOK ISBN: 978-1-4166-3117-0; see Books in Print for other formats.

Quantity discounts are available: email programteam@ascd.org or call 800-933-2723, ext. 5773, or 703-575-5773. For desk copies, go to www.ascd.org/deskcopy.

ASCD Member Book No. FY22-6 (Apr. 2022 PSI+). ASCD Member Books mail to Premium (P), Select (S), and Institutional Plus (I+) members on this schedule: Jan, PSI+; Feb, P; Apr, PSI+; May, P; Jul, PSI+; Aug, P; Sep, PSI+; Nov, PSI+; Dec, P. For current details on membership, see www.ascd.org/membership.

**Library of Congress Cataloging-in-Publication Data**
Names: Walsh, Jackie A., author.
Title: Questioning for formative feedback : meaningful dialogue to improve learning / Jackie Acree Walsh.
Description: Alexandria, VA : ASCD, [2022] | Includes bibliographical references and index.
Identifiers: LCCN 2021061127 (print) | LCCN 2021061128 (ebook) | ISBN 9781416631163 (Paperback) | ISBN 9781416631170 (PDF)
Subjects: LCSH: Questioning. | Feedback (Psychology) | Thought and thinking.
Classification: LCC LB1027.44 .W364 2022  (print) | LCC LB1027.44  (ebook) | DDC 371.3/7—dc23/eng/20220124
LC record available at https://lccn.loc.gov/2021061127
LC ebook record available at https://lccn.loc.gov/2021061128

30  29  28  27  26  25  24  23  22        1  2  3  4  5  6  7  8  9  10  11  12

# Questioning for Formative Feedback

*To Bea and Taylor Walsh, my granddaughters,*
*whose curiosity, imagination, and love of learning inspire and*
*motivate me. These are qualities I desire for all our children.*

# Foreword

When students learn, something changes within them. How does that happen? Research and practical experience show that students need to process information in order to learn, and the best way to do that is social and interactive in nature. How do people interact when they are together? They talk with one another, of course! Your thinking informs my thinking. Importantly, your thinking makes me think. If I didn't need to respond to you, I might just blip out or think thoughts unrelated to the lesson. After all, who would know, unless someone asked me what I was thinking?

In this book, Jackie Walsh shows how *quality questioning* (by both teachers and students) and *dialogue* (between and among teachers, students, and peers) serves as *feedback* that supports learning. This is a primary way in which learning happens, and that's why the title claims this feedback is *formative*.

This book includes graphic representations of key concepts and processes, tools and protocols for use by teachers or students, and classroom examples. These features are some of my favorite parts of the book. They make it easy for teachers to begin using questioning for formative feedback and hit the ground running. Ultimately, questions for formative feedback should become part of a teacher's repertoire, and questioning in some form should become the core of most lessons.

This book supports the effectiveness of this approach by citing research and providing practical examples, so I don't need to do that here. Instead, I'll try to inspire you by telling three brief anecdotes: one serious, one funny, and one from my own work as a professional developer.

Here's the serious story. Maybe 30 years ago, I was watching an episode of *Bill Moyers Journal* on public television. He was interviewing Sara Lawrence-Lightfoot, a professor at Harvard and a sociologist who studies the culture of schools. Moyers asked, "What is good teaching?"

Oh boy, I thought, what a way to put someone on the spot on national television. How can you answer a question like that in a sound bite? But she did. She replied that good teaching is "ideas conveyed through relationships." Four words that, when you think about it, are as true as they are profound. That interview, and especially those words, have informed my thinking about teaching over the course of my career.

Questioning of the sort described in this book—and especially dialogue— is a means for building relationships around ideas in a lesson. Students share their thinking and open their thoughts to others, and together the class builds meaning.

Here's the funny story. When I was in elementary school—I can't believe I still remember this, but I do—my teacher had a collection of plays for students to perform. This was back in the days when seats in rows and individual work were standard operating procedure. If we were "done" with our work before others, we were allowed to do a limited number of things, and reading was one of them. I remember reading those plays for fun during my "done time," and my favorite was a radio play titled *Inside a Kid's Head* by Jerome Lawrence and Robert E. Lee. It was a tour inside the brain of Richie, a 10-year-old student, as he sat in his school class.

My 10-year-old self thought it was hysterical, but I had to be careful not to laugh out loud because it was silent work time. It was a radio play, so there were sound effects, which I thought were clever, too. For example, there was a fast whistle that the narrator explained was the sound of some information flying in one ear and out the other. My favorite part was when the story got caught in the threads of what turned out to be "wool" as Richie was wool-gathering. The reason I thought it was so funny was because it was so true! At least for school the way I experienced it those many years ago.

Questioning and dialogue, as described in Walsh's book, change what happens "inside a kid's head." Gone are the days of 10-year-old Richie, alone with his thoughts (or lack of them). Questioning and dialogue open up students' brains, to extend the analogy, by inviting others in, clearing out the cobwebs, and rearranging the furniture.

And here's the story from my work as a professional developer. Over the last couple years, I facilitated a professional learning community for arts educators in a large school district. We were working specifically on learning targets and success criteria, not questioning per se, but what my work shares with the work described in this book is the focus on students actively working together and using the formative learning cycle (Where am I going? Where am I now? Where to next?) to further their learning and be part of a community of learners.

During one PLC meeting, I got chills. The teachers came to the realization that using success criteria supports equity in education because all students, not just some, have access to the criteria for good work. After one of the teachers said just that, everyone got excited and chimed in with their own examples, and about 20 minutes of dialogue ensued. It was an extended a-ha moment for all of us. Strategies that give access to learning to *all* students support equity in education. Questioning, dialogue, and feedback—of the sort described in this book—certainly support all learners.

I invite you to read this book and to incorporate quality questioning, dialogue, and feedback into your own teaching. In so doing, you will make changes in the lives and learning of the students in your care.

**Susan M. Brookhart, PhD**
Professor emerita, Duquesne University
Consultant, Brookhart Enterprises, LLC
Associate editor, *Applied Measurement in Education*

# Acknowledgments

This book is a testament to the power of feedback. Over the course of 35 years, I've been privileged to learn with and from teachers committed to improving classroom questioning practices. Their feedback influenced my understanding of the important connections among questioning, dialogue, and feedback—the focus of this book. My work with these teachers and their students underscored the need for intentionality in developing student capacity to question, seek and use feedback, and participate in meaningful classroom dialogue.

I am particularly grateful to the teachers and students featured in the 21 videos accessible through QR codes that provide powerful classroom visuals of these principles at work. Over the course of two years, the following teachers partnered with me in piloting the framework and many of the tools featured in this book: Kate Armstrong (1st grade) and Sue Noah (kindergarten), Athens Elementary School, Athens, Alabama; Kati Haynes and Heather Pounders, Weeden Elementary, Florence, Alabama; Samantha Hammond, Jesse Snider, and Anna Wooten (8th grade ELA), Florence Middle School, Florence, Alabama; Jane Haithcock and Leslie Sedberry (8th grade ELA), Joseph Roberts (8th grade math), and Lori Sheiler (prealgebra), Liberty Middle School, Madison, Alabama; and Mary Busbee (biology), Jessica Sutherland (chemistry), and Brad Waguespeck (AP environmental science), Vestavia Hills High School, Vestavia Hills, Alabama. Courtney Evans (math), Oxford Middle School, Oxford, Alabama, also filmed video for the book. Tracy Ray (3rd grade), DeArmanville Elementary, Oxford, Alabama, contributed her reflection on a unit designed using the principles of questioning for formative feedback.

None of this would have been possible without the active support of district leaders, school principals, and instructional partners from the participating schools and districts.

The Teaching Channel's TeachPlus provided a platform on which these teachers posted class videos over the course of a year for my viewing and feedback. This enabled reciprocal feedback regarding classroom use of the featured practices. Cheri Dedmon and Cherry Thompson of the Teaching Channel were instrumental in making this happen.

A special thank you goes to Davis Lester, Brainworks Media, for his assistance with video postproduction. Davis's artistry in editing made possible the 21 finished videos that bring to life the ideas presented in this book.

Insights from practitioners affirmed what I have learned from important thought leaders. Early in my investigation of questioning, I encountered the work of J. T. Dillon, whose extensive research and writing shaped my thinking. Dylan Wiliam added to my understanding of questioning and its connection to formative feedback. Sue Brookhart's work deepened my appreciation of the importance of developing student capacity to use feedback. John Hattie's research and writing extended my understanding of dialogue and feedback, leading me to make connections between questioning and these two. I am indebted to these and other researchers for creating a robust knowledge base that underpins my thinking.

The incubation period for this book was longer than anticipated due to unforeseen circumstances. Allison Scott, my acquisitions editor and friend, was understanding and supportive throughout the process. I am extremely thankful for her patience and unfaltering belief in the project. She is a trusted thought partner whose interest and insights made for a better product. I also appreciate the careful read and feedback provided by Jamie Greene, ASCD editor, whose attention to detail as well as big ideas contributed to consistency and clarity.

As I worked to complete this book during a challenging year, I was cheered on through weekly Zoom visits with two special friends from my undergraduate years at Duke University. I am grateful to Penny Welling, college roommate, and Marion Thompson, with whom I shared my early years of teaching, for their interest and reinforcement.

The love and support of my family—Catherine, Will, Stephanie, Bea, and Taylor—continue to motivate and inspire. Each of them energizes and adds unique meaning to all that I do.

**Jackie Acree Walsh, PhD**
Montgomery, Alabama
November 2021

# Introduction

---

*How can we harness three powerful processes to optimize student learning?*

---

Learning knows no boundaries. The potential for learning exists whenever and wherever we interact with our environment. Learning that occurs beyond school walls is usually spontaneous, occasioned by curiosity, flashes of insight, or felt needs. It results from interaction with an environment that almost always provides authentic and instantaneous feedback. By contrast, learning inside most classrooms is traditionally orchestrated by teachers who guide students through a predetermined curriculum on a fixed schedule. Too frequently, this results in passive student compliance devoid of the skill, will, and thrill associated with authentic learning (Hattie & Donoghue, 2016).

With this in mind, how can we infuse school learning with the authenticity and excitement associated with real-life experiences? One means to this end is the strategic use of quality questioning, purposeful dialogue, and formative feedback. When skillfully employed, these processes interact to increase student and teacher engagement around content and result in increases in learning for all. Together, they can create the "golden moment in learning when the context is live, the student is 'in the flow,' and the learning is gaining momentum" (Hattie & Clarke, 2019, p. 82).

## The Roots of This Book

This book explores the relationship between quality questioning and formative feedback in K–12 classrooms—and it spotlights dialogue as the bridge connecting the two. My interest in these relationships evolved from longtime work with teachers committed to the use of quality questioning, a process designed to engage all students in thinking and learning (Walsh & Sattes, 2005, 2016).

Quality questioning encompasses lesson planning, the development of student capacity as questioners and responders, and facilitation of lessons driven by quality questions. Lesson planning involves the design of questions that spark thinking and the selection of response structures that support

1

participation by all. Planning questions and selecting response structures are necessary steps, but not sufficient by themselves, to full engagement of students. Equally important is developing student understanding of the purposes of classroom questioning and of their responsibilities in the process. Additionally, the intentional use of pauses for thinking is essential when facilitating a lesson driven by quality questioning.

Based on years of work with teachers focused on improving these questioning processes, I reached the same conclusion as Wiliam (2018): "There are only two good reasons to ask questions in class: to cause thinking and to provide information for the teacher about what to do next" (p. 79). However, I add a third reason to this: to generate information for students about what to do next.

Adoption of this perspective leads to a renewed understanding of the value of questions above the recall level. No longer are questions viewed as simple tools for evaluating student recollection of facts; rather, they are understood as catalysts for student meaning-making and activators of responses that serve as feedback regarding progress toward learning goals.

Higher-level questions generate more complex student thinking, which leads to extended and elaborated speaking—a prerequisite to student dialogue. All students, however, do not come to us with the skills and dispositions required for productive dialogue. Teacher interest in helping students develop these skills ultimately led to the writing of *Questioning for Classroom Discussion* (Walsh & Sattes, 2015), which offers a framework for using questioning in the service of increased student dialogue.

Dialogue not only reveals student thinking but also results in "visible learning." Hattie (2012) exhorts teachers to move from monologue to dialogue, which has a pronounced effect on achievement ($d = 0.82$), and he notes the connection between increased dialogue and feedback, resulting in an effect size of $d = 0.75$. In addition, dialogue is a rich source of feedback to both students and teachers. In Hattie's (2008) view, "It is the feedback to the teacher about what students can and cannot do that is more powerful than feedback to the student, and it necessitates a different way of interacting and respecting students" (p. 4). This different way of interacting with and respecting students is at the heart of questioning for formative feedback.

## Challenges and Connections

Incorporating questioning that generates productive dialogue and meaningful feedback into one's practice presents several challenges. Primary among these are (1) modifying the roles and responsibilities of teachers and students in the questioning process, (2) moving from a right-answer to a deep-learning orientation, and (3) engaging *all* students in thinking and responding. These challenges require both teachers and students to change their core beliefs and accompanying classroom practices and behaviors. Addressing these challenges directly is a prerequisite for using the three processes as effective levers for increased engagement in thinking and learning, and overcoming them involves deliberate, daily work to restructure and "renorm" classrooms.

Figure 0.1 illustrates the core processes and their relationship to thinking, learning, and one another. In practice, the processes do not occur in a sequential, linear fashion; rather, they are dynamic and recursive. This dynamism is propelled by teachers and students who actively seek to create the conditions that nurture the processes.

**FIGURE 0.1**

Core Processes Associated with Questioning for Formative Feedback

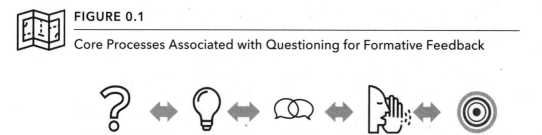

| Quality Questioning | Thinking | Dialogue | Formative Feedback | Learning |

This framework has been tested and elaborated in collaboration with teachers across five different school districts. Many of these teachers' stories (and accompanying videos) enliven the pages that follow. They illustrate the ways in which teachers can partner with students to develop classrooms where responses to quality questions provide feedback for use in determination of next steps in teaching and learning. These and other practitioners continue to inform the thinking of this author through formal and informal feedback.

## Rationale

Quality questioning, dialogue, and feedback can be strategically designed to address the needs of a new generation of learners. Skillful use of these three processes advances the academic, social, and emotional learning of all students. Brookhart (2001) found that successful students engage in self-assessment, which requires student self-questioning and internal dialogue as ongoing metacognitive processes. These are outgrowths of teacher modeling, use of quality questioning, and planned opportunities for meaningful class dialogue that scaffolds and supports individual students' thinking—and generates feedback for use in their learning.

Several common, overarching benefits emerge from the separate knowledge bases related to each of the three processes: increased achievement, heightened motivation and engagement, enhanced social and emotional development, and successful lifelong learners. These benefits are valued by educators, students, parents, and community members.

## Increased Achievement

Extensive investigations into the effective use of the three processes has resulted in compelling evidence of their impact on student achievement. Hattie's (2008) research on visible learning finds all three to have effect sizes exceeding the established hinge point of $d = 0.40$. Specific practices associated with questioning, including the use of think time and higher-order questions, have significant research bases of their own. Dialogue, with an effect size of $d = 0.82$ (Carnell, 2000), is also related to effective formative feedback. Feedback, which is the most extensively researched of the three processes, is among the most critical influences on learning (Hattie & Timperley, 2007) and disproportionately helps lower achievers, thereby serving to decrease the achievement gap (Black & Wiliam, 1998).

Because the processes are inextricably connected, intentional use in concert one with another has an even greater potential for impact. Their value is affirmed by both teacher evaluation frameworks (Daggett, 2012; Danielson, 2013) and national, state, and professional curriculum standards (e.g., Common Core State Standards [National Governors Association Center for Best Practices, Council of Chief State School Officers, 2010]; Next Generation Science Standards [NGSS Lead States, 2013]; College, Career, and Civic Life Framework [National Council for the Social Studies, 2013]).

## Heightened Motivation and Engagement

Improvement in academic achievement is linked to increased motivation and engagement (e.g., Bransford et al., 2000; Fredricks, 2014; Hattie, 2008; Schlechty, 2011). Questioning, dialogue, and feedback each has the potential to increase students' cognitive, social, and emotional involvement in their learning. For example, questioning prompts students to engage actively in thinking and make personal connections with academic content. The ensuing dialogue invites students to participate in social construction of knowledge by interacting with a teacher and peers. Finally, increased motivation among students is a key finding related to formative feedback that results from questioning and dialogue (Black & Wiliam, 1998; Clark, 2012; Hattie & Clarke, 2019; Shute, 2008). Shute attributes this to the reduction in uncertainty, "which occurs when students receive information that helps them close the gap" between an identified learning goal and their current status (2008, p. 157).

## Enhanced Social and Emotional Development

Increases in student agency and self-efficacy, which are important indicators of social-emotional well-being, are attributed to students' ability to seek and use formative feedback (e.g., Brookhart, 2017; Clark, 2012; Frey, Hattie, & Fisher, 2018; Hattie & Timperley, 2007). This is due, in part, to the relationship between formative feedback and the development of self-regulation. When learners receive and use information that enables them to move forward along a learning progression, a "can-do" attitude replaces a defeatist one. As they achieve success, they become more willing to assume responsibility for managing their learning.

## Successful Lifelong Learners and Productive Citizens

Effective questioning, productive dialogue, and authentic use of feedback are essential for the future success of both individuals and our democratic society. Regardless of the arena chosen by students following high school graduation—immediate entry to the workforce, higher education, or the military—skills in these three areas are prerequisites to success (Conley, 2008; Schmoker, 2011; Wagner, 2010).

## Classroom Artifact

### The End in Mind: Academic, Social, and Emotional Learning for ALL

Joseph Roberts, 8th grade math teacher at Liberty Middle School, introduced his students to quality questioning and student-led dialogue at the beginning of the school year. His goal was to help his students develop their capacity to interact with one another and eventually become leaders of their own learning. Over the course of the year, he supported these middle schoolers as they strengthened the skills and dispositions needed for self-direction and self-regulation, including the following:

• Using think time to listen actively to one another.
• Asking questions when needed for clarification and assistance.
• Building on one another's ideas.
• Respectfully disagreeing when they have a different way of thinking.
• Supporting one another's learning through collaborative problem solving.

As they near the end of the year, his students operate as a true community of practice, accepting responsibility for their own and their classmates' learning. They exhibit individual and collective efficacy while actively engaging in collaborative dialogue to address a focus question created by their teacher. They respectfully agree and disagree to reach a solution accepted by all. As the students sustain a productive academic discussion in an environment marked by mutual trust and respect, Mr. Roberts observes, listens, and takes notes. He intervenes only when he determines a need to recenter the dialogue.

This is the vision: preparing students to interact authentically and construct shared understandings as they might in real life.

## Recurring Themes

Running through this book are themes that serve as cornerstone beliefs. Each of these emerges from research and literature related to questioning, dialogue, and formative feedback:

- **Consequential teaching and learning are interactive.** The transmission-reception model of instruction does not involve questioning, dialogue, and formative feedback. Like Black and Wiliam (1998), the thinking behind this book begins with "the self-evident proposition that teaching and learning must be interactive" (p. 140).

- **Questioning, dialogue, and feedback cannot be separated.** Although the three processes will be separated for purposes of explication in the chapters that follow, the overriding argument is that they operate in tandem when learning is optimized. Purposeful lesson design that integrates the three processes results in coherent teaching and learning experiences in which "it is difficult to tell where one begins and the other ends" (Wiliam & Leahy, 2015, p. 129).

- **The emotional and cognitive dimensions are equally important in the use of feedback to move learning forward.** Brookhart (2017) advocates for a "double-barreled approach" to the generation and use of feedback—one that "addresses both cognitive and motivational factors" (p. 2). This thread runs throughout the literature on questioning and feedback, with an emphasis on the importance of both cognitive and affective considerations (e.g., Clark, 2014; Hattie & Timperley, 2007).

- **A primary goal of all instruction is to develop self-regulated learners.** The literature on feedback stresses its potential to develop students' metacognitive skills—more specifically, those that enable students to manage their own learning (e.g., Allal, 2018; Black & Wiliam, 1998; Black et al., 2003; Clark, 2012; Hattie & Timperley, 2007; Nicol & Macfarlane-Dick, 2006; Sadler, 2010). Belief in this principle is a precondition to full realization of the potential of the three processes.

- **Students must be partners in changing classroom practices in these areas.** None of the practices offered in this book can be used effectively without students understanding the why, what, and how of their new roles and responsibilities. Teachers cannot simply will these changes into their instruction; they must equip their students to be full partners in the changes (Walsh & Sattes, 2016).

- **Effective questioning, dialogue, and feedback don't just happen; teachers plan for them.** The premise of this book is that investment in planning and reflection outside of class prepares teachers to orchestrate effective questioning and dialogue and give and receive just-in-time feedback during instruction. Effective use of the three processes does not happen by accident. As the adage goes, what gets planned gets done.

## Parameters of This Book

Questioning and feedback present challenges across all arenas of instruction: oral and written, synchronous and asynchronous. Although most issues and some practices are common in all forms of teaching and learning, an effective change in practice requires focus. The emphasis of this book, then, is on the merger of questioning, dialogue, and feedback during active, face-to-face learning.

### Feedback, Not Assessment

This book does not address formative assessment as such but rather the qualities and uses of feedback generated by questioning and dialogue, which serve as informal assessments. The creation of questions to assess student progress toward identified learning goals is an important component of formative assessment, but the broader tenets of assessment are beyond the scope of this book.

### Verbal, Synchronous Learning

This book emphasizes the verbal exchanges between teachers and students that occur during a lesson. Questioning, dialogue, and feedback can also be executed via the written word, and some of the strategies offered in this book are transferable to that medium. In addition, some attention will be given to the facilitation of asynchronous discussions in an online environment—a context that assumes increased importance when face-to-face learning has been interrupted.

## Organization of This Book

The heart of this book is composed of three sections of two chapters each. The final chapter recaps major themes and relates them to dialogic feedback—the marriage of questioning, dialogue, and feedback.

**Part I: Framing the Processes:** Chapter 1 characterizes feedback as a reciprocal process that begins with student feedback to teachers and enables teacher feedback to students. Types and purposes of feedback are explored. Chapter 2 provides an overview of quality questioning—a four-part process that includes question design, student engagement, teacher follow-up, and sustained interactions and that results in learning for both teachers and students.

**Part II: Developing Student Capacity:** Chapter 3 provides strategies teachers can use to design and facilitate lessons that are formative in nature and continually advance student learning. Additionally, attention is focused on the nurturing of a culture that supports changed practice. Chapter 4 presents a compendium of skills and dispositions and makes the case for explicitly teaching students how to become more effectively engaged in seeking and using feedback. It also explores student self-assessment, feedback, and peer feedback.

**Part III: Designing Formative Experiences:** Chapter 5 focuses on the creation and/or selection of questions that produce feedback appropriate at different points in the learning cycle. Included are criteria for assessing questions and examples of questions that promote feedback related to surface, deep, and transfer learning. Consideration is given to planned and spontaneous follow-up questions that serve as feedback and prompt additional thinking. The role of student questions in a formative classroom is also spotlighted. Chapter 6 analyzes the use of "in real-time" questioning to secure responses from every student. This chapter also offers a menu of response structures appropriate for different contexts.

**Part IV: Advancing Engagement and Learning:** Finally, Chapter 7 offers a view of dialogic feedback that affords both students and teachers opportunities to learn through ongoing questioning and dialogue. Partnership relationships buttress this process. Students move toward self-regulation as they assume increased responsibility for assessing and guiding their own learning. "Psychologically safe" environments support social, emotional, and academic learning for all. Students use dialogue to coregulate learning in their classroom communities.

## Special Features of This Book

The intent of this book is to provide a manual of practice for educators who want to enhance classroom questioning, dialogue, and feedback. Although there is no one formula for application in all classrooms, there are tested principles and effective practices. Each chapter contains features you can use as you embark on your journey to create a classroom where everyone learns through intentional use of identified strategies and tools:

- **Blueprints:** Graphical depictions that provide coherent models of key processes and products. Each blueprint offers a holistic or big-picture view of an important component.

- **Tools:** Charts and other succinct presentations of strategies that can be used to achieve identified outcomes. Most tools are designed to support teachers in planning and enacting particular strategies. Some are intended for student use.
- **Protocols:** Special-purpose tools that provide step-by-step directions to complete an activity. As with other tools, some protocols are for teacher use; others are offered with students in mind.
- **Classroom Artifacts:** Examples of authentic classroom use. These take the form of videos, accessible via QR codes, vignettes, and teacher and student work products.

## Feedforward

Questioning, dialogue, and feedback are potential game-changers for teaching and learning. A robust knowledge base establishes the relationship of each process to student achievement. Thought leaders point to the interdependence of these processes in the creation of interactive classrooms where student engagement is high. Teachers who plan for intentional activation of each in their daily lessons enable their students to experience "golden moments" in learning on a routine basis.

In Part I, you will take a deep dive into the fundamentals of formative feedback and quality questioning and consider the relationship of each to dialogue. Keep in mind the importance of educating students about their roles and responsibilities in these processes, and imagine ways you can involve your students in cocreating a culture that will nurture increased participation in these powerful processes.

## Transferring Principles to Practice

As you complete each chapter, use this summative section to reflect on how key ideas relate to your personal situation. *What seems most important to you and for your students? How might you transfer ideas and strategies to your school and classroom? What topics merit discussion with your students?* Figure 0.2 provides suggestions for review and questions to stimulate reflection and dialogue. These chapter-ending tools can also be used to support educators engaged in an organized study of this book.

## FIGURE 0.2

Transferring Principles to Practice: Setting the Stage

| Opportunities for Practice | Questions for Dialogue | |
|---|---|---|
| | Teacher Learning | Teacher Facilitation of Student Learning |
| **Begin with the why.** Personal change rarely occurs without individual understanding of potential benefits. Review the three key outcomes on pages 4–5 to identify reasons for undertaking this personal journey. | Call to mind a current or recent class of students. Which of the identified outcomes might be most important to them at this point in their lives? What makes you say this? | Engage students in a dialogue focused on this prompt: *Think about a time when you experienced success in learning something new. What helped you keep trying until you met your goal?* |
| **Reflect on cornerstone beliefs.** Beliefs typically underpin habitual behaviors and practices and can be impediments to change. Look again at the recurrent themes (cornerstone beliefs) on pages 6–7 to assess the extent to which each currently affects your approach to teaching and learning. | • Which of these beliefs most strongly influences your teaching? Provide an example of something you do consistently because of this belief.<br>• Which of the principles, if any, is contrary to your beliefs? What causes you to disagree with it? | Use the following prompts to help students think about the extent to which they currently monitor their own learning:<br>• *Are you usually aware of how much progress you have made toward reaching a learning target? How do you know?*<br>• *How do you know when you are not on track in your learning—that you are misunderstanding a concept or procedure?* |
| **Assess relevance and importance of focus areas.** Teaching and learning are personal acts and strongly influenced by individual styles, strengths, and situations. Preview the focus areas of the upcoming chapters to identify which are most interesting to you. | • Are any of the chapters particularly appealing or exciting to you? If so, which one(s)? Why does this particular chapter speak to you?<br>• What do you hope to gain from reading and reflecting about this particular chapter?<br>• How do you hope to use what you learn from your reading and reflection? | Involve students in reflecting and talking about their level of engagement with classroom questioning. Use the questions below as appropriate:<br>• *What do you believe to be the purpose of questions?*<br>• *How often do you volunteer to speak during class discussions? What motivates you to speak? What gets in the way of your participating in class discussions?*<br>• *What kind of feedback helps you when you are stuck or confused?* |

# How do I use a QR code?

**Step 1**

Open the camera on
your device.

**Step 2**

Point the camera at the
code. The camera will
automatically scan the code.

**Step 3**

A notification with a
link will appear on
screen. Tap the link.

**Step 4**

Success!

# *Part I*

# Framing the Processes

The argument running throughout this book is that questioning, dialogue, and feedback are the trifecta of elevated student and teacher learning—that when the three are intentionally linked in lesson design and execution, they have the power to dramatically increase engagement and achievement. The chapters in Part I offer a particular perspective and approach to these featured processes.

Feedback has traditionally been understood as one-directional (from teacher to student; evaluative; affirming or corrective) and closed (rarely intended to engage the student in continued reflection, which might lead to self-correction). Initiate-Respond-Evaluate (IRE) is the term applied to this process, and it dominated classrooms until relatively recent times (Mehan, 1979).

During the first two decades of the 21st century, increased interest in and research related to the purposes of feedback challenged this traditional view. Different ways of thinking gave birth to new terms, including *dialogic feedback, sustained feedback,* and *feedback loop.* According to Sadler (2010), "Formative feedback should empower learners to become self-regulated learners" (p. 536). Chapter 1, therefore, offers a synthesis of the features of feedback that fuel and sustain learning.

A shift in the understanding of the purpose and practice of questioning goes hand in hand with a revisionist view of feedback. Questioning, as defined herein, is a dynamic, interactive practice understood by both teachers and students as a way to support learners in developing personal understandings about the content under study. As such, it differs greatly from the traditional view of questioning as a tool used by teachers to evaluate whether individual students can correctly recite specific factual information. This approach to questioning requires a shift in beliefs about its purposes; related teacher and student roles, responsibilities, and relationships; and the classroom culture that supports the process (Walsh & Sattes, 2016). Chapter 2 defines and analyzes quality questioning and the nature of the academic conversations—or dialogue—it spawns.

Dialogue is embedded in the revisionist views of both questioning and feedback. Inherent to high-quality questioning are practices designed to activate the thinking and speaking of all members of a classroom community. Feedback is dialogic by nature, given the requirement for reciprocity to the process. Thus, dialogue can be viewed as the bridge between quality questioning and feedback.

The approaches to questioning, dialogue, and feedback that permeate the pages of this book share several key features:

- **They involve multidirectional communication.** Through these processes, students and teachers function as both producers and consumers of the knowledge key to teaching and learning.
- **They move the locus of responsibility for decision making** about learning from teachers to students.
- **They reflect a constructivist view of learning**, based on the belief that learners must make personal meaning of knowledge in order to remember it and transfer it beyond the classroom.
- **They require teachers to be transparent with students** about the what, why, and how of these powerful learning processes.
- **They invite students to cocreate new ways of being together** as a community of learners.

The next two chapters offer explicit understandings of these three processes, build the case for a more intentional focus on each, and clarify the connections between and among them and their relationship to student learning.

# Feedback That Fuels Learning

*How can we use feedback to advance student learning?*

Feedback is universally understood as information a learner can use to close the gap between current knowledge and performance and a desired goal. Feedback becomes formative when teachers use it to adapt instruction to meet students' needs and help them close the learning gap (Black & Wiliam, 1998; Clark, 2012; Sadler, 1989) and when students use it to advance along a given learning progression (Brookhart, 2017; Wiliam & Leahy, 2015). Formative feedback, then, requires both teachers and students to be learners.

Effective formative feedback addresses both cognitive and emotional dimensions of learning (Hattie & Timperley, 2007; Yang & Carless, 2013). The aim is to develop self-regulated learners who generate internal feedback, respond positively to external feedback, and persist in efforts to achieve learning goals (Clark, 2012). Formative feedback is most successful when (1) students are learning and improving, (2) students are motivated and take control of their learning, and (3) the classroom culture supports the pursuit, use, and valuing of feedback (Brookhart, 2017).

Winne and Butler (1994) offer a comprehensive definition of *feedback* that encompasses ideas offered by other experts: "Feedback is information with which a learner can confirm, add to, overwrite, tune, or restructure information in memory, whether that information is domain knowledge, metacognitive knowledge, beliefs about self and tasks, or cognitive tactics and strategies" (p. 5740).

## Feedback and Learning

Feedback is an integral part of learning, and a teacher's view of learning determines the form, function, and effectiveness of feedback (Askew & Lodge,

2000; Sadler, 2010; Sutton, 2009). When learning is viewed as a one-way transmission of knowledge, students are unlikely to reflect on how the information fits in with what they think about a topic or use feedback to modify or extend their thinking. Sutton (2009) argues for replacing the "transmission-reception" approach to learning with an "engagement model" oriented to creating "dialogic learning and teaching relationships that enable students to act on the information provided by teachers" (p. 3).

Language reveals the assumptions we make. Think about the language of feedback, which includes the concept of "giving feedback," an idea consistent with the transmission-reception approach to learning. Feedback as a gift (i.e., something you give) evokes the image of a finished product conveyed to passive recipients (Askew & Lodge, 2000).

Askew and Lodge (2000) offer ping-pong as an alternative metaphor where learners are seen as active agents in building personal understandings through a back-and-forth dialogue with their teacher and peers. This constructivist view treats knowledge as something created by students as they connect new information to prior learning and experiences (Hargreaves, 2005).

A third model of learning, dubbed coconstructivism, moves beyond a constructivist focus on learning as an individual responsibility to a collaborative approach in which responsibility for learning is shared among members of a community. Knowledge is constructed through loops of information and feedback, and learning and feedback thereby become intertwined and interdependent (Askew & Lodge, 2000; Clark, 2012; Yang & Carless, 2013). Volleyball or basketball serve as more appropriate sports metaphors for this model. Coconstruction of knowledge was on full display as 8th graders in Joseph Roberts's math class collaboratively solved a problem (see p. 6).

We emphasize the ping-pong and volleyball approaches to feedback. This is not to undervalue well-constructed teacher feedback to students as a gift when it is appropriate and useful. Like all good gifts, however, effective feedback depends on interactions that provide the giver with information to support decision making about the most appropriate gift to offer. As Nicol (2010) argues, "Feedback should be constructed as dialogue between teacher and student and/or peer to peer where meaning is constructed" (p. 8).

## Feedback as a Process

Feedback addresses all domains of learning, and it is important to remember that formative feedback is a process—not an event. It is a dynamic intended to further the development of learner competence and confidence. Sawyer (2006) expresses the centrality of feedback to learning as he writes about the "new science of learning":

> Learning is a process of continuously modifying knowledge and skills. Sometimes new inputs call for additions and extensions to existing knowledge structures; at other times they call for radical reconstruction. In all cases, feedback is essential to guide, test, challenge, or redirect the learner's thinking. (p. 234)

Planning and facilitation of formative feedback is essential to effective teaching. However, there are three aspects of this feedback that help illustrate its dynamic nature and foreshadow several issues involved in planning for its effective use. Namely, feedback is dialogical, reciprocal, and cyclical.

## Dialogical

Feedback includes "all dialogue to support learning in both formal and informal situations" and, in fact, can "better be described as dialogue" (Askew & Lodge, 2000, pp. 1, 12). This type of dialogue can occur in three arenas: between student and teacher, from peer to peer, and within an individual student's mind. When it results from two-party communications, dialogue requires both participants to listen actively to each other and use what is said to reflect and revise their thinking.

The most effective kind of feedback, however, motivates students to begin an internal dialogue prompted by feedback received from others (Sutton, 2009). This involves self-questioning, a metacognitive skill that has a high impact on achievement with an effect size of $d = 0.64$ (Hattie, 2008). An important subskill related to self-regulation, self-questioning is actually a goal of formative feedback (Black et al., 2003; Clark, 2012; Nicol & Macfarlane-Dick, 2006).

## Reciprocal

The principle of reciprocity characterizes effective feedback. This is an extension of its dialogic nature. Hattie and Zierer (2017) emphasize the importance of bidirectional feedback, arguing that student feedback to teachers is more important than teacher feedback to students. They write, "Learning and teaching are dialogic processes. Successful teachers are thus capable both of giving students feedback on their learning processes and of demanding and interpreting feedback from students on their own teaching processes" (p. 75). This evokes the ping-pong image where carefully framed teacher prompts ("serves") elicit student responses ("returns") with subsequent volleying as long as the ball is in play. Keep in mind, though, that the volleying associated with feedback is collaborative—not competitive as in the case of a game.

Relationships based on mutual respect and trust are preconditions for true reciprocity. Student willingness to provide honest feedback to teachers and peers depends on a sense of safety and trust that others will respect their responses, correct or not. Their acceptance and use of feedback also depend on their emotional reactions to others. An important teacher responsibility is to engage students in cocreating a culture that supports a positive social-emotional environment in which feedback can thrive.

## Cyclical

Feedback needs to go beyond simply sharing information about student progress. For feedback to function in a formative sense, it must be used by the learner (Hargreaves, McCallum, & Gipps, 2000). In short, "Feedback is not feedback until students use it" (Wiliam & Leahy, 2015, p. 107). This process begins with the identification of a learning goal, proceeds through identification and collection of relevant data, continues with dialogic exchanges, and culminates when learners use the feedback to clarify understandings, modify strategies, or take other steps to move toward closer attainment of a learning goal. The final step closes the feedback loop and leads to the identification of a new goal.

The three feedback questions popularized by Hattie and Timperley (2007) relate to different stages of the cycle:

- Where am I going? (*Feedup*)
- How am I going? (*Feedback*)
- Where to next? (*Feedforward*)

These three questions relate to the three components of feedback: (1) knowledge of the desired learning goal, (2) evidence about current position, and (3) some understanding of how to close the gap between the two (Sadler, 1989).

## Functions of Feedback

There are two overriding purposes of feedback: to serve as information students can use to move their learning forward, and to provide teachers with information they can use to make decisions about what to do next to advance the learning of individual students and the class as a whole. Effective feedback for learning furthers both of these goals.

## Feedback Develops Student Capacity to Close Gaps

The most widely accepted purpose of feedback is to move students along a learning progression. More specifically, feedback helps them

- Reinforce and extend their correct understandings.
- Correct mistakes or errors.
- Unravel misconceptions.
- Identify next steps in learning.

Formative feedback facilitates the process of student self-assessment (Black & Wiliam, 1998; Clarke, 2000; Sadler, 2010, Sutton, 2009). Teachers support this by

- Providing tools and strategies for use in reflection and self-appraisal.
- Asking questions to scaffold self-assessment.
- Affording time and opportunity to make meaning of external feedback and apply it to one's current status.

Effective feedback reduces cognitive load (Shute, 2008). Often, students feel overwhelmed by confusion and "not knowing." They don't know where to begin. Teachers can reduce this anxiety by

- Narrowing student focus to a discrete concept or skill embedded in a learning goal (i.e., feedup).
- Providing access to evidence about one's current level of learning related to a specific goal (i.e., feedback).
- Facilitating an understanding of alternative strategies for closing the gap (i.e., feedforward).

Effective feedback reveals tacit, or "hidden," knowledge (Black & Wiliam, 2009; Clark, 2012). Tacit knowledge—knowledge developed through personal experience—influences students' thinking and is usually the basis for their (correct and incorrect) assumptions about concepts studied in school. This knowledge is usually unspoken and difficult to elicit through written assignments. Dialogic feedback has the capacity to stimulate this hidden knowledge, providing access to both the learner and the teacher.

Formative feedback enhances student agency, self-efficacy, and self-esteem (Brookhart, 2017; Clark, 2012; Sutton, 2009; Yang & Carless, 2013). When students actively participate in dialogic feedback, they can correct misunderstandings and meet learning goals. As they develop the capacity to self-assess, they become more competent and confident learners. These affective outcomes are as important to future academic success as the cognitive ones.

## Feedback Helps Teachers Make Decisions About Next Instructional Steps

If teachers want to provide feedback that serves the purposes outlined in the previous section, they must first seek and use feedback from students that helps them determine how best to support their learning.

In-the-moment feedback from one student to the teacher reveals that student's need and suggests the next instructional move to advance his or her learning. This need can often be addressed within the context of the dialogue that generated the feedback.

- If a student makes an error or mistake, the teacher can point out the source of the error and scaffold correction.
- If a misconception surfaces, the teacher can engage the student in dialogue to peel back the experiences that led to the faulty inference and help the student identify evidence or use reasoning that counters the inference.
- If a student responds correctly, the teacher can guide the student to deeper thinking and learning.

Patterns of student feedback provide information for teacher decision-making about where to go next for a class. As a teacher collects evidence related to learning, he or she can make inferences about the readiness of the whole class for alternative next steps. If a majority of students demonstrate movement along the expected learning progression, the teacher continues with the lesson as planned. However, if feedback suggests a significant number of students failed to meet the identified goal, then the teacher reteaches or provides additional practice.

Feedback also provides information to help differentiate instruction within the lesson. Teachers use in-class feedback to create ad hoc groups based on current levels of proficiency. This requires anticipation and planning prior to the class. For example, teachers may have created activities to support students who need additional practice and assignments to challenge those who have met the target. They then meet with a small group that requires reteaching.

Alternatively, they can use feedback to organize small-group peer tutoring (a powerful way to differentiate), matching students who have demonstrated proficiency or understanding with those who are not yet there. Teachers can analyze feedback collected during a daily lesson after that class and use this to pre-group students and prepare materials for differentiation in the next day's lesson as the 3rd grade teachers do in the following example.

## Classroom Artifact

### Feedback from Students Informs
### Collaborative Lesson Design

Heather Pounders and Kati Haynes, 3rd grade teachers at Weeden Elementary School, routinely use daily feedback from their students to collaboratively plan the next day's lesson. They reflect on information derived from student work products, class dialogue, and exit tickets to differentiate students who have not yet reached mastery from those who have—and they create a learning design that addresses the needs of all students. Using different data sources enables them to "catch" each student who may need additional instruction. In this video, you'll listen in as they make meaning of classroom artifacts and reach data-based decisions. You'll also take a peek inside Mrs. Pounders's classroom as she provides feedback to students based on their previous day's performance.

Harvard University Professor Eric Mazur (2013) has revolutionized feedback in his award-winning physics instruction. Dr. Mazur shifted from a teacher-centered to a student-centered model, moving from lecture and summative assessment to daily formative assessment using questions focused on key concepts. Students respond to questions using an electronic all-response system. This strategy enables him to quickly determine the percentage of students who have misconceptions. If 70–80 percent of students do not respond correctly, he reteaches. When 30 percent or more of his students respond correctly, he instructs class members to find someone who has a different answer and work out their misunderstandings to reach agreement on a correct response.

Professor Mazur's model can be adapted to upper elementary and secondary settings. The thinking behind this approach can also be modified for use with the youngest of students. This way of thinking about feedback stems from a simple principle: teachers cannot give knowledge to learners; students must work to unravel misconceptions themselves, using feedback to identify and grapple with their misconceptions.

## Classroom Artifact

### Ad Hoc Teacher-Led Small Groups:
### A Forum for Feedback

Elementary teachers frequently organize ad hoc small groups to meet with them for differentiated instruction. This practice is less frequently used in secondary classrooms. Lory Schieler, 8th grade algebra teacher at Liberty Middle School, is a great believer in this process. She analyzes data from all sources to identify students who need extra practice in identified skills and brings them together for feedback conversations. She notes that the dialogue students have with one another in this setting is perhaps more valuable than the direct reteaching she delivers. She also emphasizes that the groups are fluid and ever-changing, based on her analysis of current data. In this video, she helps four 8th grade students engage in dialogue around this focus question: *Explain to me different ways that you can solve linear quadratic systems.*

The FAR Cycle is a step-by-step approach to generating and using feedback that moves student learning forward. Developed by Nancy Love and her colleagues at Research for Better Teaching (Love et al., 2020), this framework emphasizes the action steps teachers take in response to formative feedback from their students. A brief description of this model appears in Figure 1.1.

## Features of Effective Feedback

The acid test for the effectiveness of feedback is an affirmative response to this question: *Was it used by students to advance their learning?* Wiggins (2012) calls out seven important features of feedback that work to this end: it is goal-referenced, tangible and transparent, actionable, user-friendly, timely,

**FIGURE 1.1**

## The FAR Cycle

The Formative Assessment for Results (FAR) Cycle is a four-step process that teachers implement in their classrooms and that teacher teams work on together to maximize the power of formative assessment to promote equity, achievement, and engagement.

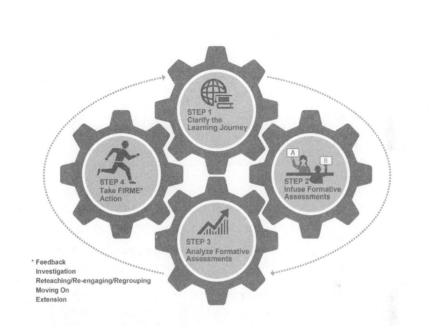

### 1. Clarify the learning journey.

The first step in the FAR Cycle is clarifying the learning journey. In this step, teachers get clear about what is essential for students to know and be able to do for each unit of study and create a progression of lesson-size targets that will lead students to mastery of the unit essentials. Then, for each lesson, teachers create student-friendly learning targets and success criteria that let students know: *What am I learning? Why does it matter? How will I know when I am successful?* What is vital in this step is that students internalize the targets and success criteria and use them to motivate, focus, and monitor their learning.

### 2. Infuse formative assessment.

In this step, teachers weave formative assessment throughout their instruction, ideally every 10 minutes, to gather evidence for the purpose of informing next steps in learning. Formative assessment can take the form of diagnostic questions or tasks combined with all-student response systems (e.g., mini whiteboards, polls, A-B-C-D cards, entrance or exit tickets), products in process (e.g., drafts of essays, lab reports, art projects), quizzes or tests with opportunity to retake, and student discourse.

(*continued*)

**FIGURE 1.1–(*continued*)**

## The FAR Cycle

**3. Analyze formative assessment results.**

This step is about analyzing formative assessment results. Teachers often do this on the fly, such as by quickly sorting entrance tickets to determine who's got it and who doesn't and then regrouping or reteaching accordingly. Alternatively, they listen carefully to student discourse for the use of academic language, for discourse skills, and for evidence of confusion or misconceptions, often using an observation checklist and intervening with probing questions or feedback on the spot. For assessments that require more analysis (e.g., projects in process), teachers—individually or with a team—analyze student work to discover which success criteria were met and not yet met, uncover patterns of errors or misconceptions, and plan for next instructional steps.

**4. Take FIRME action.**

FIRME is an acronym that stands for the five actions teachers take in response to formative assessment results:

- F stands for feedback. Most students are starved for effective feedback—the kind that causes them to think and provides specific information about what to do next. Ramping up the quantity and quality of feedback students receive, including training students to self- and peer-assess and provide effective feedback to one another, are among the highest leverage actions teachers can take to improve achievement.
- I stands for investigating student thinking. Asking students to explain their thinking and engage in academic discourse is a staple of a rigorous classroom. In a formative assessment cycle, investigation comes into play when the teacher needs to understand more about how a student is thinking about a concept or skill in order to unravel the confusion or fill in missing information.
- R stands for reteaching, reengaging, and regrouping. As we know, students learn at different rates. Teachers reteach to ensure that students who need it get another opportunity to reach the learning target. Reteaching is targeted to specific students and to the specific skill or concept they did not learn completely the first time. It often requires teachers to use a different way of explaining the skill or concept (e.g., using a graphic organizer, memory device, or analogy to connect to students' experiences). Reengaging means engaging learners in a different way (e.g., through role-play, computer simulation, peer feedback, or learning stations). Regrouping entails choosing from a repertoire of grouping strategies, such as by choice or by cooperative or flexible readiness groups.
- M stands for moving on. This is a legitimate response to formative assessment data when most, if not all, students have achieved proficiency—as long as there is a plan in place to support those who aren't there yet.
- E stands for extension. For students who master the target before others, teachers provide opportunities for extension—valuable, challenging, and rewarding learning experiences that are not simply harder tasks or busywork.

*Source:* Used with permission from Nancy Love, Research for Better Teaching, Acton, MA. Copyright 2021 by Research for Better Teaching.

ongoing, and consistent. Beyond these generalized principles, the characteristics of feedback that works vary with the stage in the learning cycle or the level of knowledge being developed. Additionally, feedback is best when it is customized to the needs of individual learners.

## Levels of Feedback

Hattie and Timperley (2007) offer a useful framework for thinking about the different types of feedback. They encourage teachers to maximize process-level feedback (level 2) and self-regulated feedback (level 3).

**Level 1: Task-level feedback.** This type of feedback is appropriately used in the early stages of learning when students are developing singular skills or requisite facts. It relates to the performance of a specific learning task such as decoding words, solving a simple equation, or responding to a recall question. This is the most common focus of feedback primarily because of the preponderance of recall-level questions in classrooms. Corrective feedback is the type most frequently provided at this level. Examples: *"That's not correct. Listen carefully as we talk more about this. I'll come back to you later to find out if you've worked through this." "You're using the wrong operation. Reread the problem again and think about how to attack this problem."*

**Level 2: Process-related feedback.** This is more effective than task-level feedback because the focus here is on how the student arrived at a response—not on the answer itself. This type of feedback is more in line with dialogic feedback, often prompting students to rethink and modify their initial responses. Chapters 2 and 5 explore how to use questions and questioning to sustain this level of feedback. Examples: *"What makes you say that?" "How did you arrive at this conclusion?" "What evidence do you have to support this inference?"*

**Level 3: Self-regulated feedback.** Given that self-regulation is a goal and potential benefit of formative assessment and feedback, this is the most highly valued level of feedback. The intent here is to develop students' ability to generate feedback for themselves. Self-regulation involves a set of metacognitive skills that are further explored in Chapter 4. Examples: *"Reflect on the steps you used to reach this conclusion. What might you have left out?" "In what ways does your response align with the success criteria?"*

**Level 4: Self-related feedback.** This level of feedback is the least useful to students because it focuses on the individual—not on their performance or work products. Included at this level are both praise and criticism. Examples: *"You are a good writer." "You do sloppy work."* Self-related feedback can be useful in nonacademic conversations as teachers develop personal relationships with their students. For example, "You really hustled in last night's game" or "I really appreciate you table manners."

## Criteria of Effective Feedback

The nature of feedback varies by level; however, a number of qualities apply to feedback in almost all contexts and stages of learning. Figure 1.2 is a tool you can use to reflect on the feedback generated in a given lesson. You may wish to record and watch a class segment to self-assess. Alternatively, you can call to mind specific feedback events and consider how, if at all, you might improve.

It's important to point out that the first criterion—aligns with learning goals—is fundamental. Other types of feedback can actually undermine student learning. Sawyer (2006), for example, points out the negative impact of praise and criticism, an undue focus on grades, and the like. These practices are most often associated with a "culture of competition" that uses grades as a carrot and where teachers and students alike embrace a fixed mindset.

**FIGURE 1.2**

Criteria for Assessing the Quality of Feedback

| Criterion | Suggestions | Level of Feedback |
|---|---|---|
| **Focus** | | |
| Aligns with learning goal | Connect feedback to the learning target, calling specific attention to it as appropriate. | • Task-level<br>• Process-related<br>• Self-regulated |
| Narrows attention to one step of thinking or problem solving or to a bite-sized concept | Direct learner's attention to a singular mistake, error in thinking, or concept for further analysis. | • Task-level<br>• Process-related<br>• Self-regulated |
| Falls within students' zone of proximal development ("sweet spot") | Connect follow-up questions or other scaffolds to prior learning when supporting students in rethinking errors or misconceptions—or in extending understandings. | Process-related |
| Connects to prior knowledge | Reinforce and build on correct understandings. | • Task-level<br>• Process-related |

| Criterion | Suggestions | Level of Feedback |
|---|---|---|
| **Focus–(*continued*)** | | |
| Addresses the performance, not the person | Direct comments to either the deficit or the exemplary aspect of the performance, not to the individual. | • Task-level<br>• Process-related |
| **Function** | | |
| Provides missing information | Offer cues or clues to assist with retrieval of factual information. Reteach when evidence suggests a high percentage of the class lacks essential skills or requisite knowledge. | Task-level |
| Sustains thinking | Use questions or statements to prompt student rethinking of a response, identify an error, provide evidence, or deepen understanding. | • Process-related<br>• Self-regulated |
| **Tone** | | |
| Is nonjudgmental | Avoid both criticism and praise; use descriptive language. | • Task-level<br>• Process-related |
| Is caring and supportive | Communicate in an attentive, thoughtful, and sensitive manner, using both nonverbal cues and voice tone and tenor to convey care. Demonstrate sensitivity to individual students' social-emotional needs. | • Task-level<br>• Process-related<br>• Self-regulated |
| **Wording** | | |
| Uses clear and explicit word choices | Select words that are explicit and unambiguous. | • Task-level<br>• Process-related<br>• Self-regulated |
| Is succinctly worded | Employ sentence structure that is straightforward. | • Process-related<br>• Self-regulated |

A primary responsibility of teaching is to intentionally integrate opportunities for formative feedback into daily lessons. Chapter 2 makes a case for quality questioning as the premier process to achieve this end, Chapter 5 examines requirements for questions that activate and sustain dialogue to produce this feedback, and Chapter 6 focuses on structures and strategies to hold all students accountable for participation. The quality questioning process and its constituent practices are the facilitators of formative feedback, and feedback is an important end game of dialogue.

All this being said, how can teachers frame their role as designers and activators of feedback in a manner that conforms with the qualities laid out in this chapter? Figure 1.3 offers a framework for organizing thinking about this important responsibility.

**FIGURE 1.3**

Blueprint for Designing and Orchestrating Formative Feedback

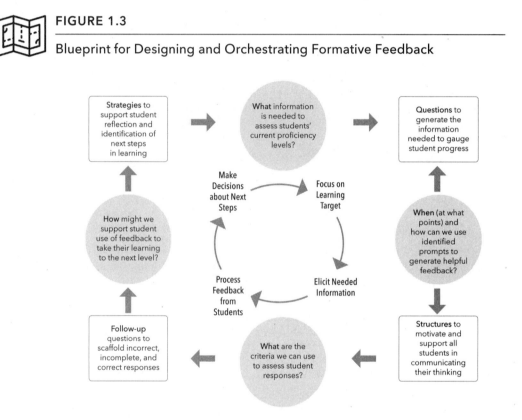

Key: Circles = Planning Questions; Rectangles = Products for Classroom Use

The nucleus of this blueprint is a four-stage cycle illustrating the actions teachers take during a lesson to generate and use feedback. Although the stages are presented sequentially, the specific actions associated with each stage are recursive and dynamic—as is all of effective teaching.

- **Focus on learning target.** Gaps in learning cannot be discerned without ongoing references to the learning goal, which is the lodestar for feedback. In formative classrooms, learning targets are visible, transparent, and understood by all. Teachers use these during lesson design to form quality questions and other prompts and during instruction to gauge student progress.

- **Elicit needed information.** Teachers pose questions and other prompts during class to stimulate student thinking and sharing of responses that serve as feedback. This is done at multiple points in a lesson through the use of a variety of planned and spontaneous prompts.

- **Process feedback from students.** Thinking through a student's response is a complex process that involves making meaning of her comments and questions, comparing them to expected responses, and making inferences about an individual's or an entire class's current level of knowledge and proficiency.

- **Make decisions about next steps.** Inferences inform a teacher's next steps. Will you provide feedback in the form of follow-up questions or will you reteach, offer additional practice, or move on with the lesson? How can you support students' ongoing self-assessment and goal setting?

This process cannot effectively occur unless teachers have intentionally planned in advance with each stage of the process in mind. The blueprint features four critical questions to guide planning:

- **What information is needed to assess students' current proficiency levels?** Planning for formative feedback begins with identification of the various "need to know" points embedded in daily learning targets. These become the focus for questions and prompts to activate student thinking. Wiliam (2011) refers to such questions as hinge point questions defined as questions designed in advance "to check whether students are ready to move forward" (p. 101).

- **When (at what points) and how can we use identified prompts to generate helpful feedback?** Teaching involves the back-and-forth of structuring information and soliciting feedback from learners. Identifying the points in a lesson where we can integrate preplanned quality questions is essential to productive outcomes. Selecting response structures and other strategies to engage all students is another critical part of planning explored in Chapter 6.

- **What are the criteria we can use to assess student responses?** Identifying expectations for an acceptable response before class prepares teachers to make in-the-moment inferences about a student's current level of understanding. Also invaluable is advance thinking about how

to proceed when responses reveal possible errors in thinking or erroneous preconceptions.

- **How might we support student use of feedback to take their learning to the next level?** We cannot leave student development of metacognitive skills to chance. Without these, self-regulation—the most
valued outcome of formative feedback—will not occur.

---

## Classroom Artifact

### Multiple Forms of Feedback
### Emerge During Literature Circles

Anna Wooten, 8th grade ELA teacher at Florence Middle School, seeks and
uses feedback from her students to decide her next steps in instruction,
whether in the moment of their learning during class or in the planning
of future lessons. She also realizes the benefits of student-student feedback and of opportunities for individual learners to reflect and self-assess,
thereby generating self-feedback. Mrs. Wooten believes literature
circles provide the intimate setting supportive of these multiple
forms of feedback.

Literature circles offer Mrs. Wooten the opportunity to listen in to
student conversations and use that dialogue to ascertain individual
progress toward meeting standards. She can also distinguish between students who have mastered the curriculum standards and those who are still
struggling to do so. Additionally, this structure encourages peer feedback
as students share and compare insights based on textual evidence. In her
reflection, she also notes the feedback she collected on her lesson design,
including affirmation of the choice of response structure and insights
related to how she might craft questions of even higher quality.

---

## A Framework for Student Engagement

Teachers can meticulously design and purposefully move through the feedback cycle. If, however, actions do not have a formative effect on learning, it is
not feedback (Sadler, 1989; Wiliam & Leahy, 2015). The dialogic nature of feedback requires students to engage in specific behaviors throughout the process
to ensure that learning occurs.

Six discrete action steps increase the probability that students will have the ability and motivation to use information generated in feedback conversations. Figure 1.4 presents these steps as a cycle powered by a combination of metacognitive and verbal moves teachers can explicitly teach students.

**FIGURE 1.4**

Framework for Student Use of Feedback

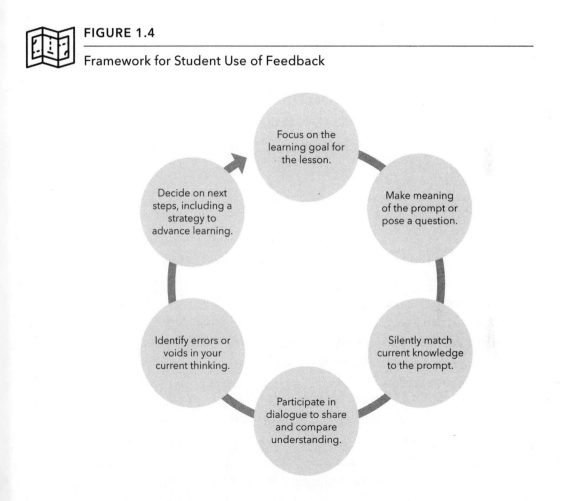

1. **Refocus on the learning goal for the lesson.** All learning sequences begin when individuals return to the target for the learning. This initial step is critical if learners are to incorporate self-assessment into the process.
2. **Make meaning of the prompt or pose a question.** Formative sequences are stimulated by a teacher or student posing a question. To become

engaged in metacognitive and verbal responses to such stimuli, students attend to and translate the prompt into words they understand.

3. **Silently match current knowledge to the prompt.** This move is also a metacognitive one. Students search their current knowledge and experience base to identify matches—and then bring those to working memory for easy access in public interactions.

4. **Participate in dialogue to share and compare understanding.** This is the step that occurs in a community setting and requires active listening and reflection. The heart of the dialogic feedback process—the back-and-forth—may involve an individual student responding to the teacher, listening to peers' responses, or questioning and responding to peers. A nonnegotiable aspect of these interactions is that students feel comfortable publicly sharing what they think they know and posing questions when confused. Concurrently, students compare their current thinking to that offered by others.

5. **Identify errors or voids in current thinking.** A teacher can help a student pinpoint an area of confusion or missing skill/knowledge, but only the learner can accurately identify the exact point of misunderstanding in their progression toward proficiency. The learner's job is to verify the missing link before deciding on the next best step to take—along with the most appropriate strategy to use.

6. **Decide on next steps, including a strategy to advance learning.** This is the culminating action in the cycle and often requires coaching from the teacher or a peer. It enables the student to reach the learning goal and move to the next level.

Some students automatically move through this cycle, whereas many others lack the knowledge and skills to do so on their own. One responsibility of teachers who commit to enhanced use of feedback is to explicitly teach students the *what* and *why* of this cycle—and help them develop the skills to complete each action. Use the graphic in Figure 1.4 to help your students understand the importance of this process. Chapter 4 offers strategies for helping students develop associated skills.

The framework can scaffold student participation in formative experiences, providing them with a map to use as they navigate the learning landscape. Other practices accelerate and add value. These include being open and honest with the teacher about their level of understanding, proactively seeking help when stuck, and responding to peers with open and honest feedback when engaged in collaborative learning. When students learn skills and dispositions associated with quality questioning and dialogue, they are better able to initiate feedback moves—to seek and offer feedback—rather than being passive recipients of teacher information.

## Feedforward

Both teachers and students benefit when they become more intentional in seeking and acting on feedback. Teachers' use of feedback enables them to become more precise and strategic as they make decisions about how to help individuals and groups of students move their learning forward. Students who are savvy users of feedback can assume greater responsibility for their own learning as they improve their performance. Understanding the functions and features of effective feedback contributes to better planning and use of quality questioning to generate this valuable commodity for learning. The next chapter details the features of quality questioning that enhance the surfacing and use of feedback by all members of the learning community.

## Transferring Principles to Practice

Use Figure 1.5 to reflect on how key ideas presented in this chapter relate to your personal situation. What seems most important to you and your students? How might you use the tools included in this chapter to advance the quality and use of feedback and to interact with colleagues about these topics? What topics merit discussion with your students?

**FIGURE 1.5**

Transferring Principles to Practice: Feedback That Fuels Learning

| Opportunities for Practice | Classroom Applications | |
|---|---|---|
| | Teacher Learning | Teacher Facilitation of Student Learning |
| **Approach feedback as an interactive process.** Formative feedback, unlike evaluative feedback, engages learners in reflecting on their responses—correct or incorrect. Consider the dialogic, reciprocal, and cyclical nature of feedback. | Intentionally use pauses to reflect on a student's response and formulate a follow-up question to get behind or extend their thinking. Engage in dialogue with the student to learn more about why they are responding as they are and to provide feedback that will scaffold their thinking. | Use the following focus questions to engage students in dialogue: <br> • *Why might it be important for you to respond to a question when you are not certain you are correct?* Help students understand that their responses—correct or incorrect—provide you with insight into where they are in their learning. <br> • *How do you feel when I ask you a question about a response you have given?* Let students know that the purpose of your follow-up questions is to learn more about how they are thinking about a problem or concept—not to embarrass them. |
| **Reflect on how feedback enables you to be more effective in your teaching—and on how it supports students as learners.** Review the different ways in which feedback supports students and teachers. | Prior to a selected lesson, create differentiated lessons for (1) students whom you identify as needing additional practice in a skill or concept, (2) students ready to extend or take their learning deeper, and (3) students who need reteaching. Use formative feedback to identify these three groups during the lesson and form ad hoc groups addressing each condition, if appropriate. | Begin a dialogue with students by asking the following question: *Feedback is my response to you after you respond to a question. What do you believe to be the purpose of my feedback? How does this help you learn?* Tapping resources that can be adapted to the age group you teach, help students better understand the ways in which feedback can support their learning. |

| Opportunities for Practice | Classroom Applications | |
| --- | --- | --- |
| | Teacher Learning | Teacher Facilitation of Student Learning |
| **Consider each of the four dimensions of effective feedback (as shown in Figure 1.2).** | How might you use the identified criteria to assess the current quality of your feedback to students? In what ways might you use these criteria to plan for more effective feedback? | Plan another conversation with students about the purposes and features of feedback. Consider using the following question to prompt their thinking about the type of feedback they find most useful: *What is more helpful to you as a learner: (1) having someone give you the "right" answer, or (2) having someone ask questions that help you discover your error and figure out the correct response yourself? What makes you say that?* |
| **Talk through Figure 1.3.** Seek to understand the three components of the figure—the steps, planning questions, and products—and their relationship to one another. | Use this model to plan for feedback that you might deliver in an upcoming lesson. If possible, plan with colleagues who will be teaching the same lesson. | Use the inside portion of the figure (the cycle) to help students understand why their honest responses to your questions are important. Reinforce the idea that responses to questions—even when students are not certain of their correctness—provide important information to help you teach better. |
| **Assess the potential value of the framework for student engagement.** Use Figure 1.4 as a tool for teaching students how to seek and use feedback. | Engage in dialogue with colleagues about the value of helping students better understand their role in seeking and using feedback. Consider the extent to which your students currently use feedback and how you might work schoolwide to develop knowledge and skills in this area. | Plan a minilesson to engage students in thinking about how to become better seekers and users of feedback. Use Figure 1.4 and related explanations as resources for planning. |

# Questioning That Generates Dialogue and Feedback

---

*What features make questioning "quality," thereby generating dialogue and feedback?*

---

Questioning is a process that can potentially elicit student thinking and speaking to provide teachers with the data (i.e., feedback) necessary to form effective feedback for students. Questioning can be the activator of dialogic interactions that produce reciprocal feedback when it meets criteria associated with "quality." Adopting practices associated with four functions of quality questioning is a potential game changer for learning.

Traditionally, questioning has been viewed as something teachers use to guide students through a lesson and determine if they are on track and paying attention. This model, commonly called IRE (initiate-respond-evaluate), is rooted in teacher control and student accountability. Low-level, factual questions dominate, a small percentage of students respond, and questions are asked in a rapid-fire manner. Feedback is equated with a teacher's evaluation of students' answers regarding their "correctness." This approach places students in a passive, submissive role and treats each teacher–student exchange as an isolated event. It is not grounded in the reciprocity that makes feedback truly formative.

Quality questioning (Walsh & Sattes, 2005, 2016), a dynamic and interactive process, is a counter to IRE. The most important difference is the expectation that students assume an active role at each stage of the process. A second distinction relates to student responses, which are viewed as verbal expressions of their current thinking about the focus of the question—not as right or wrong answers. As teachers listen to and interpret students' responses, they gain insights into where students are in their learning so they can provide helpful feedback, often in the form of follow-up questions. Cognitive and social-emotional engagement, not accountability and compliance, are the overriding purposes of quality questioning.

Viewing the questioning process through this lens requires a change in both teacher and student beliefs about the purposes of questioning and its component parts—along with an acceptance of new roles and responsibilities. Figure 2.1 illustrates the core functions associated with questioning that activates thinking to produce feedback that is useful to teachers and students. These functions help organize and explain the new beliefs, purposes, and practices essential to the effectiveness of questioning for formative feedback.

**FIGURE 2.1**

Questioning to Generate Thinking

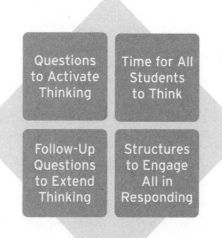

## Questions to Activate Thinking

Questions can serve as catalysts for thinking, which in turn enables students to participate in dialogue that generates useful feedback for all members of the classroom learning community. To serve this end, teachers must craft questions with this explicit purpose in mind. A second prerequisite for dialogic feedback is that both teacher and students understand and embrace this overarching purpose of questions.

Quality focus questions give birth to thinking, dialogue, and feedback. Teachers prepare a limited number of these questions prior to a lesson for the explicit purpose of generating student feedback to use in guiding instruction. These questions activate student thinking that leads to initial responses, which lead to various types of follow-up questions—another core function of the quality questioning process.

## Characteristics of Focus Questions

Focus questions center and stimulate student thinking at critical junctures in learning. Such questions call attention to factual, conceptual, or procedural knowledge that students have had an opportunity to learn and that is essential for students to move to the next level of learning. One of the most important decisions teachers make as they design a lesson is the focus (i.e., facts, concepts, procedures) and placement of these questions (i.e., when exactly to pose them). Each daily lesson incorporates a limited number of focus questions, which are strategically prepared in advance. The appropriate number varies by subject area and stage in the learning cycle, but in general, one to four such questions are sufficient.

Focus questions must meet four conditions, each of which contributes to the question's effectiveness at promoting intended outcomes. They must

- Align with the learning goal.
- Be appropriate to learners' needs and interests.
- Contribute to feedback about student learning.
- Be clear and understandable.

**What knowledge and cognitive skills do students need in order to attain the current learning goal?** The first step in the preparation of a focus question is careful examination of the "where to" in learning. The proximate learning goal is the related daily learning target (DLT), and each focus question should connect to an identified DLT. Almost all DLTs warrant a related focus question. Teachers may also benefit by returning to the curriculum standard and unit goal from which the DLT was derived. This enables validation of the substantive importance of the DLT, spotlights academic language, and places the knowledge in a broader context. Alignment of the question with this learning outcome is essential to producing feedback that moves students along a learning progression.

**How will students receive the question?** Vygotsky's (1978) zone of proximal development (ZPD) is an important tool for determining the cognitive appropriateness of a question. The ZPD represents an appropriate level of challenge for students: the level just beyond current mastery (i.e., the level they can handle with support from their teacher or peers). Some call this the "sweet spot" of learning, a task challenging enough not to bore but not so difficult as to frustrate. This is the learning space that will be most productive for the greatest number of students in a given class. Questions within the boundaries of a group's ZPD can potentially engage almost all students, representing a range of progress across the identified zone.

However, academic readiness is not the only indicator of learner appropriateness. Linking a question to the background experiences and interests of students connects to prior knowledge and motivates thinking. Think about how a question might be crafted differently for students living in a rural area versus those living in a city. Sensitivity to social-emotional factors is another important consideration in the crafting of focus questions. Quality questions meet students where they are both socially and emotionally. They engage students and invite them to make connections to what they already know about the topic.

**What evidence of student learning is the question likely to produce?** Put another way, how do you imagine your students will respond? This is an important question teachers ask themselves as they prepare and craft focus questions. Anticipating student responses is helpful in the fine-tuning of questions. Is a given question likely to generate misconceptions and errors in addition to complete and correct responses? Effective focus questions uncover errors in thinking and serve as reference points for scaffolds (including follow-up questions), which help students correct misunderstandings and move forward in their learning.

**Will students understand what is being asked?** Wording is important. Sentence structure makes a difference. If students cannot understand a question, they cannot form a response. Many classroom questions are asked aloud, affording students practice in listening to understand. This is an important skill. However, if the question is long or complex, asking aloud while projecting it on a whiteboard is appropriate. Offering students a written version of the question concurrent with asking it can also be an important practice in classrooms with English language learners.

The need for clarity is yet another argument for crafting questions in advance. It is good practice to ask the questions out loud and ask a colleague if they make sense (i.e., are clear and understandable). Conceptualizing these questions can be challenging, but effective communication of the "asks" we pose to students is essential.

## Purpose of Questions

Changing classroom questioning patterns begins with a return to basics. Ask students *why* teachers pose questions, and most will respond that it is to find out if students know the right answer or if they are paying attention. How would your students respond?

If questions are intended to yield valid feedback, then students need to move away from this mindset. "Right answers" and accountability are what most students associate with school questions. Instead, students need to understand that questions are intended to activate their thinking and support their learning. Related to this is the recognition that errors in thinking can be opportunities for everyone to learn (Black et al., 2003; Hattie & Timperley, 2007).

Providing students with opportunities to discuss the purpose of the questions they are being asked is a first step toward supporting the development of new beliefs. Figure 2.2 offers specific guidelines that can focus such a discussion. Simply announcing these guidelines is not sufficient. Students need to make meaning of them and fit them into their view of themselves as learners.

 **FIGURE 2.2**

Teaching Students the Purpose of Questions

> ➤ Use questions to think about what you know, not to guess the teacher's answer.
>
> ➤ When a teacher asks a follow-up question, reflect on what you said and modify or add to your initial thinking.
>
> ➤ Ask questions of your own when you are confused or need clarification.
>
> ➤ Ask questions of your own to express curiosity or find out more about the subject.

One strategy for reinforcing new norms is to change the language of learning. Typically, teachers talk about "questions and answers," but what if we talk with our students about our interest in their *responses*—not our *answers*—to our questions? It is important to explain that you are interested in their thinking and response to a given question, not in a predetermined answer.

For these new guidelines to make sense to students, questions must be "worth thinking about." A constant barrage of recall questions (i.e., those that require simple regurgitation rather than deeper thinking) will undermine this norm. Similarly, responses to recall questions are of limited value to teachers; they only reveal whether students remember facts and information—not whether they understand. "The only way to obtain more powerful formative feedback is through posing questions that matter" (Duckor & Holmberg, 2017, p. 79). Framing focus questions in the manner previously described increases the probability that powerful formative feedback will result. In addition, collaborative planning enhances the quality of questions, and collaborative reflection on students' responses enables teachers to collectively decide where to go next.

## Time for All Students to Think

Time for All Students to Think

When questions activate thinking, students need time to engage in cognitive processing. However, research has consistently found a pattern of fast-paced question-answer sequences across all classrooms. Rowe (1986), while investigating student questions in science classrooms, first brought attention to this pattern and coined the term *wait time*. Her research uncovered two critical points in the question-response sequence when pauses can be effectively used: immediately after asking a question (and before calling on a student to answer) and just after a student responds (but before providing feedback or recognizing another student to speak).

Limited time to think precludes most students from participation and results in superficial dialogue (Black et al., 2003). As a result, the traditional question-answer sequence fails to produce information about where most students are in their learning (Black & Wiliam, 1998). When students learn to use strategic pauses to think, the quality of the feedback provided through their responses is more accurate and complete. Getting students accustomed to silence can, however, be daunting. Indeed, most have become comfortable with an IRE pattern after years of use and find it difficult to adjust to new routines.

Many of us learned about wait time during a college course, and many teachers have tried to introduce it to their students—with limited success. Because of the potential for wait time to influence the quality of feedback you receive through student responses, I recommend partnering with students to make it work in the classroom. One suggestion is to adopt the term *think time* in lieu of *wait time*. The former communicates an expectation that students use the pause to actively *think*—not just wait. Another challenge is to help students understand the *why* of think time and what specifically they should be thinking about during the pauses. To begin, we must consider what thinking actually requires us to do.

## What's Involved in Thinking

One of my earliest memories of school is being asked by my 1st grade teacher, Mrs. Gaines, to put on my "thinking hat." I assumed she meant, "Try to come up with the right answer." It didn't occur to me that more might be involved in thinking than simply recalling what she had taught us. In all fairness to Mrs. Gaines, *cognitive science* was not a term commonly used in the mid-20th century, and *metacognition* had not yet entered our vocabulary. Today, however, we not only have access to a substantial knowledge base about thinking, but we know that metacognition, when used effectively, can be one of the most powerful levers for increased achievement (Hattie, 2008).

How, then, can we invite students into a discussion about thinking? One approach is to share a graphic representation and walk them through the process. Figure 2.3 provides a tool you can use for this purpose. This model is adapted from the work of cognitive scientist Daniel Willingham (2009) who calls it "the simplest ever model for how thinking works" (p. 11).

Consider using this tool as a metacognitive lens through which students can consider why they need time to think. Engage them in reflecting and talking about this visual representation. The sequence of such a discussion (the wording of which can be modified for young learners) might go something like this:

- Teacher points to *Input from External Environment* on the graphic and says, "As we engage in classroom interactions, one of our jobs is to listen actively to questions that focus our attention on learning goals."
- Teacher continues by calling attention to *Working Memory* on the graphic and asks, "Do you know what working memory is? [Pause for discussion, then continue with explanation.] When we attend to a

question, we bring it into our working memories to translate and use in searching our long-term memories."

### FIGURE 2.3

Tool for Teaching Students About Thinking

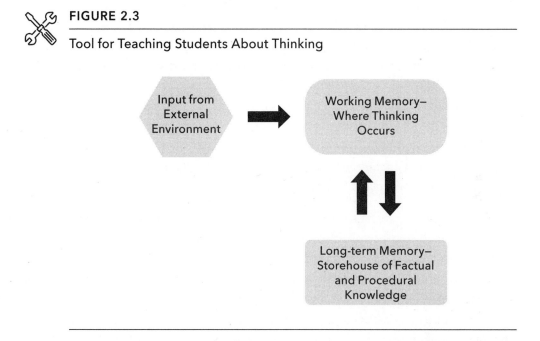

- Teacher asks students to reflect on this question: "What do you think might be involved in 'translating' a question? Why might this be important?" Teacher asks students to turn and talk to partners to exchange their thoughts and then share what their partners thought.
- Teacher moves focus to *Long-term Memory* on the graphic and says, "This is where we file our personal knowledge and experiences. Bits of information are connected by synapses to other related bits. Each of us has a unique set of connections, which cognitive scientists call our schema. Schemas are frameworks for organizing and interpreting the information we have stored. A question can prompt us to look around our schema for a match, which we bring back to our working memories. Can you remember a time when you were searching for information? What helped you succeed in your search?"
- Teacher points out the double arrows on the graphic and suggests the back-and-forth process between working and long-term memory:

"After bringing information to our working memory, we can engage in cognitive processing using the thinking verb in the question. For example, some questions call on us to analyze information."

- Teacher stops and asks, "What does the verb *analyze* mean to you?" Teacher pauses (think time 1) then names someone to share. Teacher invites other students to agree with, disagree with, add to, or otherwise comment on the initial response.
- Teacher continues by saying, "As we continue, we may retrieve additional information from long-term memory."
- Teacher brings the presentation to a close by inviting students to respond to the following with a thumbs-up if they agree or a thumbs-down if they disagree: "Most of us need more than one second to engage in the thinking required to respond to a question." Teacher asks students to be ready to explain their responses.

Most students conclude that time is needed to respond to questions. They also usually agree that different individuals require varying amounts of time to move through the process. This is a good point at which to introduce another new norm: no hand-raising to volunteer a response to teacher questions. Help students understand that the waving of hands interferes with others' thinking and can cause many people to stop thinking because they believe someone else will answer for them. Hand-raising is an artifact of "right-answer" oriented classrooms in which students (and teachers) believed the primary purpose of questions was to get the right answer on the floor as quickly as possible. (We will return to this norm in Chapter 6.)

## Think Time 1

Think time 1 refers to the pause immediately following the asking of a question. Rowe's (1986) research revealed 3–5 seconds as the threshold for a pause sufficient to produce desired outcomes. Among these outcomes are three that have relevance to the production of dialogic feedback: (1) lengthier, more cognitively complex responses; (2) a higher percentage of students, including low achievers, participating; and (3) an increase in the number of student questions.

**Lengthier, more complex responses.** Hattie (2012) reports that students' answers to questions are usually very brief with only two to four words (70 percent of the time). This is a function of both the low cognitive demand the questions require and the absence of time to think—practices that support each other. By contrast, responses to higher-level questions, followed by sufficient time for all to prepare a response, are more elaborate and complete, and they provide richer and more accurate feedback to teachers. Ultimately, this enables the formation of more substantive and supportive feedback for students. Deeper thinking requires time.

**A higher percentage of students participating.** Another benefit associated with the use of think time 1 is an increase in the percentage of students participating in classroom dialogue. This increase is particularly notable for low-achieving students. This outcome is critically important for the generation of feedback sufficient to make informed instructional decisions. Many teachers opt for written assessments because of a felt need to obtain responses from the maximum number of students (and because they believe only a few students are willing to respond verbally). Think time—in combination with strategically selected response structures—provides equitable opportunity for all students to engage in dialogue. When afforded with the time to think and the chance to participate actively, all students' confidence increases, contributing to greater self-efficacy.

**Increase in the number of student questions.** The impetus for Rowe's (1974) research leading to the "discovery" of wait time was the infrequency of student questions in science classes. In a groundbreaking study of 103 classrooms, Rowe found only two in which academic questions were asked and in which teachers employed a strategic use of pauses. This finding motivated additional research, which led to the identification of several benefits, including an increase in student questions (Rowe, 1986; Tobin, 1986). Student questions are not only a source of rich feedback but also drivers of classroom dialogue, which produces feedback to the questioner and other students. (Chapter 5 offers insights into other strategies for encouraging students to form and ask questions aloud.)

Teachers and students benefit from consistent use of think time 1. Teachers who have successfully integrated this pause into their classroom routines are more likely to ask fewer questions of higher quality, expect more from lower-achieving students, and provide more thoughtful feedback (Rowe, 1986; Tobin, 1986). This three- to five-second pause also provides teachers with time to be thoughtful as they seek to secure valid feedback *from* students and improve the quality of their feedback *to* students.

During this pause, teachers can silently consider three important questions. The first, asked while scanning the class to "read" students' nonverbal reactions, is *Do most students appear to understand the question?* If looks of confusion persist after five seconds, the teacher might ask one student to restate the question. Usual practice is for teachers to restate the question themselves even before three seconds have elapsed. Asking a student to restate the question has a number of advantages. It encourages active listening, provides an opportunity for students who haven't understood to hear the question in a peer's words, and affords the teacher a chance to clarify what is being asked.

The second question for teacher reflection is *What will an acceptable response sound like? What are the knowledge and cognitive requirements?* Effective feedback helps students close the gap between what they currently know (as expressed in their response) and the learning goal. This requires an almost instantaneous comparison of a student's actual response to the expected one.

Finally, the teacher determines *How will I call for the response?* Often, this is a choice between naming one student to respond (and deciding which student) or creating an opportunity for all students to express their thinking (e.g., think-pair-share, initial electronic response). Decisions about response structures are best made during lesson planning; however, on occasion, teachers may sense a need to make a change in what was planned to meet an emerging need. Teacher thinking completed during the first pause affects the quality of the feedback exchanges that follow.

Changing long-established, deeply rooted practices is difficult for students and teachers alike. How do teachers succeed in incorporating the first pause into class routines? Begin by acknowledging that this cannot be done without student understanding and commitment, which require students to be clear about the purpose of the pauses. Once done, this can prepare students to consider a new classroom norm: *Everyone needs time to think to prepare their best response to a question.*

## Classroom Artifact

### Establishing New Norms to Support Thinking and Dialogue

ELA team members Samantha Hammond, Jesse Snider, and Anna Wooten share their experiences in teaching 8th grade students the *what* and *why* of new questioning norms. These teachers give testimony to the power of eliminating hand-raising as the go-to method of respondent selection and address how to deal with high-achieving students who may be resistant to this policy. They also share how they scaffold the use of think times 1 and 2 during the early months of a school year to the point that they become part of the fabric of their classroom cultures as the year progresses. Their dialogue and classroom examples provide insights into these questions: *Why is it important to teach new norms for responding? What has worked for us as we've sought to partner with our students to embed these norms in our classroom cultures? How do these norms support enhanced thinking by all students?*

Once students know the *what* and *why* of think time 1, they become more receptive to learning how to use the pauses. I suggest that teachers outline and model four specific metacognitive behaviors to help students respond more correctly and completely (Figure 2.4). As students move through the four steps, they respond to the indicated questions, which convert into self-questions that can prepare them for a response.

## Classroom Artifact

### Intentional Use of Think Times
### Transforms Classroom Talk

Mary Busbee, biology teacher at Vestavia Hills High School, uses quality questioning strategies as she engages her students in learning biology. She works with her students to cocreate a collaborative, open, respectful classroom culture in which thinking and participation by all are invited and expected. This recorded lesson features small-group and whole-class dialogue focused on the cell communication. Both Mrs. Busbee and her students demonstrate consistent use of think times to ask and respond to questions and to process responses as feedback for learning.

As she reflects on her use of think times and other quality questioning strategies, Mrs. Busbee notes the benefits to her students and her own learning. She credits think time and the use of collaborative groups with engagement of traditionally reluctant students. Both practices contribute to a safe environment in which students can grapple with challenging questions.

**FIGURE 2.4**

Teaching Students How to Use Think Time 1

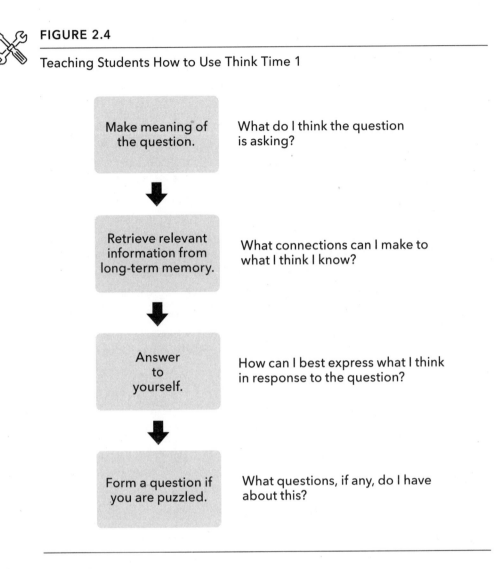

| | |
|---|---|
| Make meaning of the question. | What do I think the question is asking? |
| Retrieve relevant information from long-term memory. | What connections can I make to what I think I know? |
| Answer to yourself. | How can I best express what I think in response to the question? |
| Form a question if you are puzzled. | What questions, if any, do I have about this? |

## Think Time 2

The pause following a student's response to a question is the space in which dialogue can emerge. During this time, everyone in the classroom community is expected to reflect on what was said and be ready to talk about the response. This includes the responding student, other classmates, and the teacher, each from a unique perspective. The threshold for an effective second think time is (as for the first) three to five seconds. At times, a longer pause is appropriate. However, in reality, this second pause is almost nonexistent in many classrooms because of interruptions.

Initial research on the second think time focused on benefits to the responding student (Tobin, 1986). Among those identified, the ones with greatest impact on the quality of feedback are these:

- Student responses are often longer and more complete.
- Students provide more evidence for their responses.
- Responding students often engage in higher levels of thinking.
- Students more frequently self-correct.

More robust, elaborate responses provide teachers with greater insight into a student's thinking—be it correct or incorrect—and more information to use in moving the student's learning to the next level. In addition, the opportunity to reflect and continue speaking without interruption provides the responder with opportunities to continue thinking out loud and, in the process, become more self-regulating.

As with think time 1, students must understand the purposes and procedures for the pause. One entry to such a conversation is to ask students what the word *thoughtful* means to them. Usually, two ideas emerge. One includes words such as *considerate* and *respectful*; the other consists of *reflecting* and *thinking deeply about something*. Affirm to students that there are two different meanings of this term and that think time 2 involves both. On the one hand, it is polite and considerate to pause after someone finishes speaking. Think time 2 serves this function. On the other hand, pausing after someone completes a statement provides everyone with a chance to reflect on what was said. Think time 2 serves this function, as well.

The term *think time* is descriptive of what everyone should be doing during the pauses. In short, the expectation is for speakers to use three to five seconds to reflect on their responses and modify them if desired. Figure 2.5 shows the specific self-questions students can use for this reflection. Walk students through this graphical depiction, using an example to illustrate each step. Consider reproducing this graphic and posting it in a prominent place in the classroom.

In traditional classrooms where hand-raisers dominate, many students believe teachers are satisfied when one student provides a correct answer. They judge it safe to tune out. If called to react to a peer's response, most students (who in all likelihood did not have time to form their own initial responses) are usually unable to do so. Because they are unequipped to participate in class dialogue, they opt out. Not only does this diminish the value of any dialogue that might occur, but the rushed pace of questioning can have a negative impact on many students' self-confidence and efficacy.

**FIGURE 2.5**

Teaching Students How to Use Think Time 2

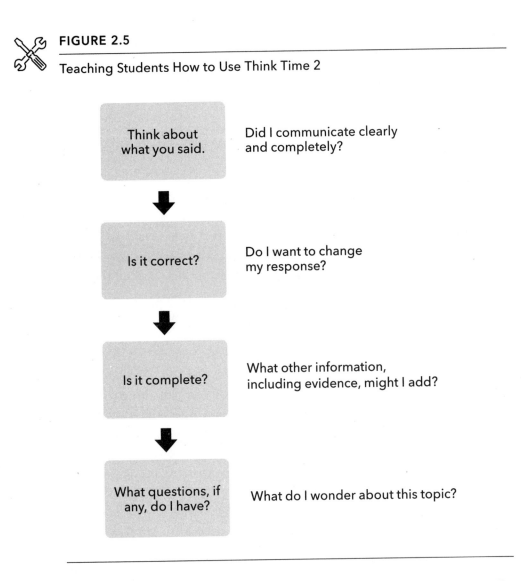

| | |
|---|---|
| Think about what you said. | Did I communicate clearly and completely? |
| Is it correct? | Do I want to change my response? |
| Is it complete? | What other information, including evidence, might I add? |
| What questions, if any, do I have? | What do I wonder about this topic? |

Teach students that think time 2 is for listeners and speakers. This is an opportunity to emphasize the importance of active listening and the value of learning from peers. With that in mind, Figure 2.6 is a graphic that can be used to underscore the expectation that all students—not just the speaker—use think time 2.

Teachers find the second think time to be more challenging for them and their students. Why is this? Many teachers learned the benefits of immediate feedback in a preservice course and interpreted that to mean split-second feedback. Others say, "We don't have time to wait. We have curriculum to cover." In fact, only one minute is required to pause the requisite three to five seconds for 12–20 student responses or comments. In light of the research related to think time's positive impact on learning and achievement, it's worth rethinking these views. Think time does not waste classroom time; rather, it's a good investment in learning that sticks.

The real challenge is changing long-established habits, especially among students. This does not happen overnight but requires a commitment to explicitly teaching and reinforcing new skills over the long haul. Remember, you can't do think time to students. Instead, you can teach them what to do during the pause, consistently honor the silence, model its use in your own behavior, and reinforce the practice daily.

**FIGURE 2.6**

Teaching Students How to Use Think Time 2 When They Are Listeners

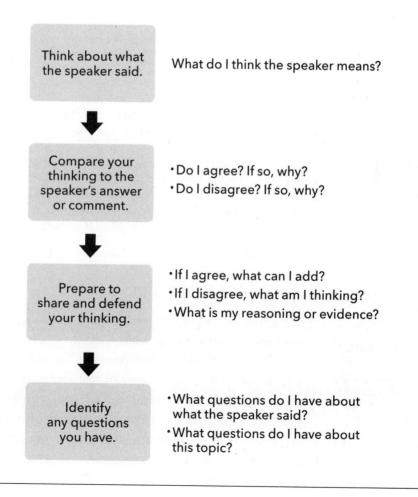

When students learn the reasons for the pauses, they begin to appreciate and use the silence to advance their learning. Even young students can learn to use pauses to think about the question and what they know. One 3rd grader expressed it this way: "When you have time to question yourself, you can come up with something that you think matches the question. If you didn't have think time, you'd have to rush and guess."

## Classroom Artifact

### Students Reflect on the Value of Think Times

Six high school students reflect on the value of think times to their individual and collective learning. Responding to focus group questions at the end of the school year, they agree that this practice transformed the culture of their class. One student credits the use of think times and the dialogue it enabled with "bringing us closer together as a class," a comment with which his peers agree.

As they engage in collaborative dialogue, the students identify specific benefits that correspond with what researchers, beginning with Mary Budd Rowe, have discovered—including opportunities to think more deeply about a concept, self-assess and self-correct, and hear from classmates who typically have not volunteered to speak in class. Students also talk about the value of a no-hand-raising policy, the freedom to voice their thoughts even when uncertain of their correctness, and their ability to use classmates' comments as feedback to advance their own learning.

## Structures to Engage All in Responding

Structures to Engage All in Responding

The third component of the quality questioning framework focuses on response structures. These are the strategies and protocols teachers select to scaffold speaking and listening in a community of learners. Strategically selected response structures serve three primary purposes: (1) to ensure that all students are accountable for thinking and speaking, (2) to help students benefit from the thinking and knowledge of their classmates, and (3) to provide the teacher with feedback from individual students and the entire class.

Hand-raising is the traditional response structure, one that still dominates in many K–12 classrooms. It is also one of the first "going-to-school" behaviors students learn. That is not a coincidence. Hand-raising is a signal to ask permission to speak or pose a question and is defensible as a classroom management routine. The question is whether it is effective as a structure for determining who speaks during a lesson. My view is "almost never."

Wiliam (2011) argues that when we allow hand-raising to be the primary determinant of who speaks during class, the achievement gap widens. We know that when we rely on volunteers to respond to questions, a large percentage of students end up never speaking. Ultimately, hand-raising does not further any of the three purposes previously identified.

So what are some alternatives to this well-established routine? Response structures can be sorted into three categories: (1) all-response systems, (2) pair-response structures, and (3) protocols for responding within collaborative groups.

All-response systems call for every student to offer an individual response. Included in this category are signaled responses, which are particularly popular with elementary teachers; work samples, including student displays of responses on a whiteboard or via an electronic option; and choral responses, which are appropriate in lessons using drill and practice to develop automaticity. A key benefit of this type of response structure is the requirement that each student think and explicitly share his or her response. These structures are most appropriate when the learning target focuses on the development of surface knowledge.

The most widely used pair-response structure is think-pair-share, which provides students with individual think time to form responses, invites partners to exchange thinking, and culminates with sharing and comparing as a whole class. This and other pair structures have the advantage of providing time and space for every student to think and share responses orally. When students are able to speak and listen to one another, to make their thinking visible, their comprehension and achievement increase (Michener & Ford-Connors, 2013). The key to the success of these and other collaborative structures is the provision of explicit directions regarding who talks when and for how long. Pair responses can serve a variety of instructional purposes, ranging from clarification of new learning to preparation for a whole-class discussion related to deepening of learning.

Other collaborative response structures involve small groups of students (usually three to five) that collectively address a question through exchanging perspectives, piggybacking on one another's ideas, posing questions to one another, and inquiring together. Response structures in this category are most useful for organizing and guiding small groups engaged in discussions, collaborative problem solving, and other pursuits usually intended to deepen learning. To avoid a potential pitfall of group work, collaborative structures provide protocols or step-by-step instructions to govern who speaks when and for how long.

Response structures from these three categories can be mixed and matched within a given lesson to optimize the number of students responding. Chapter 6 offers guidelines for different groupings of students (e.g., whole class, collaborative small groups) and different levels of learning (e.g., surface, deep/transfer knowledge).

## *Classroom Artifact*

### Preparing 8th Graders for Whole-Group Discussion

Leslie Sedberry, a teacher at Liberty Middle School (Madison, Alabama), plans for intentional use of questioning strategies as she seeks to level the playing field in class discussions. She selects quotes from *The Outsiders* by S.E. Hinton to drive discussion in her 8th grade ELA classroom. Two of Mrs. Sedberry's goals are to increase the number of students actively engaging in whole-class discussion and to promote more careful listening among her students. To accomplish the first goal, she organizes small groups so students can engage in collaborative dialogue in preparation for whole-class discussion. She reinforces the use of think time during whole-class dialogue to encourage students to listen and process one another's comments and to give her the opportunity to reflect on student responses and prepare feedback.

## Follow-Up Questions to Extend Thinking

Follow-Up
Questions
to Extend
Thinking

The fourth component of the blueprint is key to the facilitation of dialogue. Follow-up questioning is the move on which we are focusing here; however, in some instances, another teacher move may be more appropriate. For example, if a focus question reveals limited student knowledge, "reteaching" or additional individual practice may be the best move.

Follow-up questions are a preferred format for feedback to students since they transfer responsibility to the learner. Three sources of follow-up questions are (1) teacher questions, planned in advance of class in anticipation of common misconceptions or errors; (2) student questions, created by students in response to an explicit request from the teacher; and (3) emerging questions, which evolve spontaneously and organically during the flow of a lesson and may come from students or the teacher.

## Teacher-Prepared Follow-up Questions

Teachers plan these questions in advance of a lesson for possible use following an anticipated student response to a focus question. During lesson planning, collaborative teams or individuals anticipate different ways in which students might respond to a given focus question. They know the value of planning for misconceptions, which Hattie and Clarke (2019) call "the essence of feedback" (p. 31). Teachers craft follow-up questions based on their knowledge of common student errors or misconceptions related to the content of the question. One of the values of collaborative planning is the pooling of multiple teachers' experiences related to common misunderstandings.

Follow-up questions serve to make visible the student thinking that led to a particular response. Teachers use this information to scaffold student thinking and understanding and thereby support student self-correction. These questions are most effective when they are designed to address a probable misconception or error in thinking that is specific to a particular discipline. There are, however, generic questions that can be used across disciplines.

The nature of a student response determines the type of follow-up question to pose. Six common types (along with an example question for each) include

- Incomplete but partially correct responses (e.g., Could you say more about [the correct concept included in answer]?)
- Incorrect due to a careless error (e.g., Reflect on what you just said. Can you identify the error?)
- Incorrect because of faulty reasoning (e.g., How did you arrive at this conclusion [or answer]? Please walk us through your thinking.)
- Incorrect and reflecting a misconception or incorrect assumption (e.g., What makes you say [the incorrect assumption]?)
- Correct but lacking evidence (e.g., How can you support this statement?)

- Correct and open to deeper analysis or interpretation (e.g., Can you compare this to [a previously studied concept]?)

Notice that this list does not include follow-up to responses reflecting a complete lack of understanding. Follow-up questions should be posed with the expectation that students are able to say something in response. If they have inadequate surface knowledge or appear to have no idea how to proceed, a follow-up question may not be appropriate feedback. In these instances, reteaching is most likely required. Hattie and Timperley (2007) remind us that feedback "is most powerful when it addresses faulty interpretations, not a total lack of understanding" (p. 82).

All six of these examples generate dialogue of varying lengths and complexity. Depending on the initial speaker's response, ensuing dialogue may be limited to brief exchanges between the teacher and speaker. This initial exchange, however, may prompt other students to join in with comments or questions. This is the expectation—that follow-up questions open up conversation among multiple students, affording the teacher the chance to listen for additional student feedback. Such dialogue also creates the situation referenced in an earlier chapter: feedback and learning become intermingled as students listen to peers, compare their thinking to their classmates', and self-correct or extend their learning.

Jiang (2014) found that the use of follow-up questions to extend time dedicated to processing different ideas led students to deeper, less-superficial thinking. He also found that the use of follow-up questions to reveal different ideas contributed to a safe classroom environment in which learners were willing to take risks and offer different responses, even when uncertain of their correctness. When teachers show respect for their students' responses by posing questions to get behind their thinking, students come to believe their teachers are less interested in "right" answers and more interested in student learning.

## Student Questions

When cultivated and nurtured, student questions can be one of the most authentic and helpful types of feedback to teachers since they convey specific gaps in student understanding (Walsh, 2021). Regrettably, these questions are largely absent from most classrooms. But they do not have to be. Teachers can build intentional "timeouts" for thinking and question formation into their lesson design, or they can call timeouts on the fly when they notice puzzled looks or sense a need for student processing and reflection. In either event, the teacher should ask students to reflect and record their questions, which may be used as exit tickets or additional sources of immediate feedback. Some teachers have their students record questions in their journals so they can refer to them later. Regardless of the strategy used, the act of writing out a question is important in helping students clarify their thinking.

## Emerging Questions

A final type of question includes those that arise spontaneously and organically during instruction in reaction to a student's response to a question or comment. These may be initiated by either the teacher or students. Ideally, we want to provide students with the skill and motivation to ask these questions more routinely.

Well-designed follow-up questions have the potential to transfer responsibility to students in two different manners. First, the questions may prompt the initial speaker to self-correct—not just wait for the teacher or a peer to provide an acceptable response. Next, the ensuing class dialogue can generate comments and questions that enable students to learn from one another. Chapter 5 provides more specific guidelines and strategies for generation and use of all four question types highlighted in this chapter.

# Feedforward

Black and colleagues (2003) assert that "good assessment for learning involves a two-way dialogue between the student and the teacher, each not only listening to what the other is saying but using what is said to inform the learning process" (p. 89). They also maintain that effective formative feedback involves opportunities for students to think about their learning and express their learning verbally. Quality questioning nurtures and sustains this two-way dialogue. Two components of quality questioning require thoughtful and strategic advance planning. We will return to these in Chapter 5, which is focused on the framing of questions, and Chapter 6, which is dedicated to the selection of response structures.

The value of viewing dialogue as a primary generator of feedback relates to its enabling students "to initiate or respond to the teacher [so they can] detect and correct misunderstandings and ambiguities on a timely basis" (Clark, 2012, p. 209). This requires students to assume new roles and responsibilities based on accompanying mindsets and skills. Developing student capacity in these areas is the focus of the next two chapters.

## Transferring Principles to Practice

Use Figure 2.7 to compare your and your students' current understanding and use of questioning to the principles embedded in quality questioning. Which of the practices and skills seem most important to you and for your students? How might you use the tools included in this chapter to advance the quality and use of questioning? How might your students modify their current mindsets to participate more productively in quality questioning?

**FIGURE 2.7**

Transferring Principles to Practice: Questioning

| Opportunities for Practice | Classroom Applications | |
| --- | --- | --- |
| | **Teacher Learning** | **Teacher Facilitation of Student Learning** |
| **Assess current questioning patterns in your classroom.** Reflect on the opening pages of this chapter, which contrast quality questioning to the traditional question-response sequence known as IRE. Does this distinction correspond with your experience—with what you've learned about differing questioning practices? | Record a lesson segment during which questioning is the dominant instructional method. Replay to chart the question-response pattern, focusing on the following:<br>• The average number of teacher-student interactions per focus question asked.<br>• The average number of words per student response.<br>• The nature of teacher follow-up questions after student responses (e.g., evaluative or scaffolding). | • Continue conversation with students about the purposes of questioning. You might consider role-playing two different approaches to questioning—first using the IRE model and then employing the quality questioning model.<br>• Ask students to reflect on the difference between the two, specifically how they felt when their response was evaluated as to its correctness compared to when you attempted to get behind thinking and scaffold more correct or elaborate thinking. (Be prepared for students to prefer IRE, the more familiar mode. Drill down to challenge their thinking about what is really involved in learning.) |

| Opportunities for Practice | Classroom Applications | |
| --- | --- | --- |
| | Teacher Learning | Teacher Facilitation of Student Learning |
| **Think through Figure 2.1, Questioning to Generate Thinking (p. 37).** As you revisit this graphic organizer, speculate about the interdependence of the four components. How do they interact with and influence one another? | Refer to the recorded lesson segment to identify the component(s) of the blueprint that may have been underutilized in this lesson. Speculate as to why you and your students may not be using this practice more consistently. | Which of the four components do you believe students need to know more about in order to engage in deeper thinking? How might you facilitate student learning in this area? |
| **Assess your current use of the three identified question types.** Each of the three identified question types—focus, follow-up, and student—plays a distinct and important role in learning. Understanding the purposes of each, and planning for their regular use, contributes to a formative learning environment. | With colleagues in your PLC or grade-level team, discuss the extent to which you currently plan for inclusion of the three question types in daily lessons. Consider the value of being more intentional in planning for each. | Talk with students about the three question types to help them better understand how each can support their learning. Ask students to reflect individually on the extent to which they currently use each type to guide their learning. |
| **Commit to more intentional use of think times 1 and 2 with your students.** Incorporating regular and intentional use of the two think times into daily lessons can be challenging. This requires planning and direct instruction. In your view, what contributes to this challenge? | Model the use of think time as you facilitate daily lessons. As you initiate this intentional practice, use think-alouds to convey to your students what you are doing during the pauses. For example, you might say, "I paused to provide each of you with time to think about what the question is asking and to prepare your response." | Prepare minilessons to introduce the use of the two think times to students. Prepare large wall charts to display how they should use each of the pauses; that is, the kind of thinking in which they should engage when pauses occur during class interactions. |

*(continued)*

**FIGURE 2.7–**(*continued*)

Transferring Principles to Practice: Questioning

| Opportunities for Practice | Classroom Applications | |
|---|---|---|
| | **Teacher Learning** | **Teacher Facilitation of Student Learning** |
| **Connect the use of think time 2 to the formation and use of follow-up questions as formative feedback to students.** Look back to the discussion of follow-up questions and think about ways in which they might be supported by the use of think time 2. | In a given lesson, intentionally use think time 2 to engage in the following metacognitive moves:<br><br>• Make meaning of the speaker's response. What exactly did the student say?<br>• To what extent did the speaker include both the requisite knowledge and the expected level of cognitive processing in his or her response?<br>• What question might I ask to help the student clarify, correct, or extend his or her thinking? What is the most tactful way to word this question? | Encourage students to use think time 2 to form questions of their own. In the case of the speaker, the question might be one he or she has about the subject (e.g., focusing on the meaning of a term or an area of confusion). Listeners can be encouraged to pose questions that either provide the speaker with an opportunity to clarify his or her thinking or provide a rationale for the response. |

# Part II

## Developing Student Capacity

Questioning for formative feedback requires that students, like teachers, believe learning results when they are actively engaged in building their own understandings. Many students are acculturated to the transmission-reception approach and lack the skill and will to assume this new role and related responsibilities. The capacity to do so relates to both cognitive and affective dimensions. The goal here is to help students develop the competence, confidence, and commitment required for the transformed role.

Most students need explicit instruction to adopt a new process for learning. Chapter 3 provides a road map for teachers' use in creating experiences and a classroom culture that support students on this journey. Teacher commitment to the work rests on beliefs and supportive mindsets—and on the willingness to adopt new practices. As such, the next chapter explores three specific roles and related responsibilities: teacher as designer of formative lessons, teacher as facilitator of classroom interactions, and teacher as culture-builder.

Chapter 4 examines student roles and responsibilities in a formative learning environment—namely, student as self-assessor, student as knowledge constructor, and student as community member. These roles function in tandem with the teacher roles laid out in Chapter 3. One of the teacher's primary responsibilities is to help students grow into these new roles.

This chapter also explicates the skills and dispositions students require to engage actively and productively in quality questioning, dialogue, and formative feedback.

# Teacher Beliefs, Roles, and Responsibilities in the Formative Classroom

---

*What does it take to help students develop their capacity to provide, seek, and use feedback?*

---

Questioning and dialogue to produce formative feedback require a dramatic change in the way most students approach learning in school. Teachers alone cannot transform the processes associated with dialogic feedback. They must be intentional in bringing students on board and in emphasizing the *why* of the new practices.

Teachers also require clarity regarding shifts in their own ways of thinking about their roles and related responsibilities. What shifts in thinking are required? How do these shifts affect their roles and responsibilities?

## Shifts in Thinking

Reporting on their work with teachers to implement formative practices, Black and colleagues (2003) note the need for "changing the way a teacher thinks about their teaching and their view of their role as a teacher" (p. 80). This foreshadowed Hattie and Zierer's (2017) argument about the importance of mindframes, which they define as "the way teachers think about what they do" (p. xiv).

Richard Elmore and colleagues at Harvard Graduate School of Education (City, Elmore, Fiorman, & Tietel, 2009) popularized the concept of the instructional core as an organizer for thinking about instruction and the roles of teacher and student. They argue that improvement results when teachers and students interact with one another and with the content. In their view, it is the quality of the interactions that is important. Figure 3.1 is a graphical display of how questioning for formative feedback maps onto the instructional core.

**FIGURE 3.1**

Questioning for Formative Feedback and the Instructional Core

**Student**

- T poses questions to elicit Ss responses as feedback about level of S proficiency.
- Ss respond to make their thinking visible (not to "guess" the answer).
- T and Ss use pauses (i.e., think times) to listen interpretively.
- T poses follow-up questions to scaffold S thinking.
- Ss respond to one another as well as to the teacher.
- T transfers control/ responsibility for learning to Ss.
- T and Ss cocreate a safe, respectful learning environment.

- Ss use T questions to retrieve what they think they know about content.
- Ss connect prior knowledge and experience to content under study.
- Ss formulate questions to enhance understanding of content.
- Ss use T questions and feedback to adjust schema.
- Ss self-regulate progress toward learning goals.
- Ss deepen their knowledge of content as they engage in dialogue and construct new relationships.

**Teacher** ⟷ **Content**

- T formulates questions aligned with content standards.
- T uses feedback loop to position questions within students' ZPD.
- T forms questions with cognitive demand sufficient to ensure S processing of content knowledge that leads to retention.
- T anticipates probable S responses, including misconceptions.
- T forms follow-up questions to scaffold Ss toward content mastery.

In short, the teacher interacts with (1) the content to form a question and fashion appropriate feedback and (2) students to pose questions, receive and interpret responses, and offer feedback. In turn, students interact with (1) the content as they translate questions and form responses and (2) the teacher and one another as they respond and pose questions of their own. The quality of classroom interactions depends on both teacher and student values and behaviors (City et al., 2009). These interactions are rooted in a shared understanding of the purpose of questions, the value of all students being engaged, the importance of pauses for thinking, and the value of formative feedback—along with the vision for moving responsibility for regulation of learning to students.

To enact dialogic feedback as presented in this book, teachers must shift from values underlying traditional approaches to instruction to those that are compatible with an interactive classroom (see Figure 3.2). Teachers must also support students in making corresponding shifts.

## FIGURE 3.2

Shifts Associated with Use of Dialogic Feedback

| Traditional | Transformed |
| --- | --- |
| Covering Content ⟶ | Meeting Student Needs |
| Maintaining Control ⟶ | Partnering with Students |
| Presenting Content ⟶ | Facilitating Student Interactions |
| Eliciting Right Answers ⟶ | Surfacing Student Thinking |

**From covering content to meeting student needs.** This is the most fundamental—and perhaps most challenging—of the value shifts associated with dialogic feedback. Who among us has not thought, "I taught it; they just didn't learn it!" District pacing guides continue to send the message that covering the curriculum is a teacher's primary job. Everyone knows, however, that content coverage often occurs without learning. Quality questioning helps address this dilemma. By framing focus questions aligned with power standards and daily learning targets, teachers address the big ideas in the curriculum. When used in tandem with the principles of formative feedback, student learning needs become the priority.

**From maintaining control to partnering with students.** Teachers are the designated authority figures in classrooms. This is a necessary condition for the maintenance of order and discipline. The issue here is whether this principle supporting classroom management can be effective in the sphere of teaching and learning. I argue that the two are not necessarily compatible. Quality questioning requires "changing the locus of control, of letting go and allowing students to take over responsibility for progress of the lesson" (Black et al., 2003, p. 83). If we accept as our goal the transfer of responsibility to students, then we must teach them how to exercise that responsibility. This requires learning new skills and developing new dispositions that are prerequisites to interactions with the content. (Chapter 4 takes a closer look at the specific skills and dispositions needed by students to assume partnerships in their learning.)

## *Classroom Artifact*

### Developing Norms and Procedures with "Littles"

Athens Elementary School teachers Sue Noah (kindergarten) and Kate Armstrong (1st grade) reflect with their instructional coach, Anna Underwood, on establishing norms, procedures, and a safe culture for young students. They collaborate to identify the best procedures to use with their young learners. In this conversation, they stress the importance of visual cues and share the tools and strategies they use to reinforce expected behaviors with their students.

**From presenting content to facilitating student interactions.** Key to the operation of the instructional core is student interaction with content so they achieve a specified level of proficiency. Teaching as performance does not enable these interactions. This is the purpose of student dialogue. As students speak, they further their individual understandings. As they listen to one another and their teacher, they test their understandings and learn from different perspectives. Effective planning and use of follow-up questions is a primary responsibility of teachers who aspire to become successful facilitators of student interactions with content and one another.

**From eliciting right answers to surfacing student thinking.** Feedback thrives on misconceptions and errors (Hattie & Clarke, 2019), yet most students are reticent to respond to questions or speak in class if they are uncertain of the correctness of their thinking. Before convincing students that we are interested in their responses—right or wrong—we must first hold this value ourselves. This is contrary to what many of us learned as students and in our early years of teaching. I clearly remember the words a mentor shared with me during my first year of teaching: "Be careful about letting wrong answers get on the floor. Students may remember these." This led me to call on students whom I believed would answer correctly and to quickly correct those who answered incorrectly. This, of course, is completely contrary to what I deeply believe today.

Reflecting on long-held values that underpin how we teach is an important step. The concept of *mindframes* adds another dimension to the importance of teacher thinking about practice. Hattie and Zierer (2017) identified 10 mindframes that emerged from Hattie's visible learning research (Hattie, 2008). Three of these relate directly to the subject of this book:

- "I give and help students understand feedback and I interpret and act on feedback given to me."
- "I engage as much in dialogue as in monologue."
- "I build relationships and trust so that learning can occur in a place where it is safe to make mistakes and learn from others." (p. xv)

Mindframes are deeply embedded in teacher thinking and serve as a GPS to guide in-the-moment decision making. They embody how teachers think about their tasks and about why they do what they do.

The remainder of this chapter focuses on teacher responsibilities that support the development of students' capacity to participate in dialogic feedback. Adoption of the three identified mindframes will contribute to effective discharge of these responsibilities.

## Teacher Roles and Responsibilities

Teachers must assume three primary roles if they wish to develop the capacity of their students to engage in dialogic feedback. Figure 3.3 shows these roles as a three-legged stool. Failure to address one of these responsibilities leads to unsuccessful outcomes. The previously identified values and mindframes are infused into each.

**FIGURE 3.3**

Teacher Roles and Responsibilities in the Formative Classroom

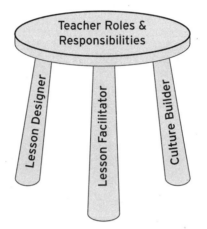

Too often, classroom observers make inferences based only on what they see occurring during a lesson. They fail to look behind the proverbial curtain and see two important determinants of lesson effectiveness: prelesson design work and ongoing creation (with students) of a learning culture. Successful use of quality questioning for formative feedback during a lesson depends on the discharge of these three critical roles and responsibilities in a purposeful and consistent manner.

## Lesson Designer

Student engagement in formative activities occurs when teachers plan for this to happen. This requires teachers to assume the role of designer of daily lessons, which involves strategic selection and positioning of key strategies requisite to student generation and use of formative feedback through dialogic processes. Figure 3.4 displays five steps and related success criteria to guide design efforts.

**Prepare focus question.** This step begins with revisiting the learning goal to identify knowledge and skills that will be the focus of the questions prepared in advance. Because the quality of focus questions determines the quality of ensuing dialogue and feedback from students, the importance of thoughtful preparation cannot be overstated. Moreover, the focus question

## FIGURE 3.4

Steps in the Design of a Formative Lesson

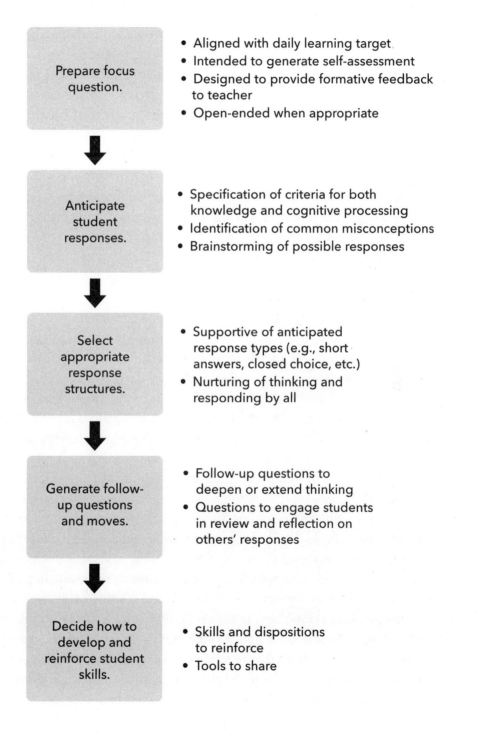

**Prepare focus question.**
- Aligned with daily learning target
- Intended to generate self-assessment
- Designed to provide formative feedback to teacher
- Open-ended when appropriate

**Anticipate student responses.**
- Specification of criteria for both knowledge and cognitive processing
- Identification of common misconceptions
- Brainstorming of possible responses

**Select appropriate response structures.**
- Supportive of anticipated response types (e.g., short answers, closed choice, etc.)
- Nurturing of thinking and responding by all

**Generate follow-up questions and moves.**
- Follow-up questions to deepen or extend thinking
- Questions to engage students in review and reflection on others' responses

**Decide how to develop and reinforce student skills.**
- Skills and dispositions to reinforce
- Tools to share

drives the other four steps in the process. (Chapter 5 focuses on the preparation of focus and follow-up questions.)

**Anticipate student responses.** One strategy for "testing" the quality of a question during the design process is to talk with colleagues about the criteria for an acceptable response. This involves stipulating both the knowledge requirements and the expectations for cognitive processing. If this is difficult for teachers, it may mean the proposed question is either lacking in clarity or flawed in some other manner. Consequently, a revision may be necessary. In addition to assessing whether a question will lead to a desired outcome, generation of an expected response has inherent value. It enhances a teacher's ability to assess a student response and offer helpful feedback during real-time classroom exchanges. During this step of the design process, it is also beneficial to generate incorrect or incomplete responses you might hear, especially those that involve common misconceptions. Doing so helps you plan for possible follow-up questions, the fourth step in the process.

**Select appropriate response structures.** This step is second only to question preparation in its importance (and is the subject of Chapter 6). The two primary criteria for choice are the extent to which the structure is likely to afford all students the opportunity and motivation to respond and the extent to which the structure will accommodate the features of the expected response.

**Generate follow-up questions and moves.** One reason teachers default to evaluative feedback is the challenge of developing complex, on-the-spot feedback. Think time 2 affords a brief pause for interpreting a student's response and determining feedback, but three to five seconds is not sufficient time to complete complex cognitive operations. Therefore, planning for feedback in advance can pay rich dividends during class.

**Decide how to develop and reinforce student skills.** Developing student capacity is a journey that requires teaching and constantly coaching students on new skills and practices. Suggestions for instruction are presented throughout this book. It is therefore important to build instruction and reinforcement into daily lesson plans. Otherwise, these skills and practices can slide by the wayside. One specific example is student understanding of the metacognitive moves associated with think times. If students are to improve their use of these skills, they need periodic opportunities to reflect on their progress and reinforce their understandings. Given the potential impact of metacognition on student performance, each daily lesson should include reinforcement of at least one relevant (to the lesson) skill or practice. The best way to ensure this happens is to build it into your lesson plan.

The work of collaborative teams is greatly enhanced by incorporating question preparation and planning for feedback into lesson planning efforts. Figure 3.5 relates key design functions to the four guiding questions recommended by DuFour and Eaker (1998) for the work of PLCs.

**FIGURE 3.5**

**Connecting Questioning for Formative Feedback to Four PLC Questions**

**What do we want all students to know and be able to do?**
• Prioritize and unpack standards.
• Formulate learning targets.
• Prepare quality questions.

**How will we know if they learn it?**
• Agree upon the criteria for a correct and complete response, including both the knowledge and cognitive dimensions.
• Identify response structures that engage **all.**
• Plan to use think time 1 and think time 2 to allow time for processing and recalling.

**How will we respond when some students do not learn?**
• Anticipate student misconceptions and errors.
• Prepare follow-up questions to get behind thinking that may have led to incorrect thinking.
• Prepare follow-up questions to scaffold thinking and move students toward a complete and correct response.

**How will we extend the learning for students who are already proficient?**
• Prepare follow-up questions to take thinking deeper.
• Plan enrichment tasks to deepen or extend learning.
• Plan opportunities for these students to engage in peer tutoring.

Design work benefits from collaborative thinking and dialogue. Figure 3.6 provides a template corresponding to the design process that can be used during collaborative planning in PLCs or team meetings.

## Learning Facilitator

Teachers who assume the role of learning facilitator seek to transfer the locus of control for learning to their students. To this end, they focus on explicitly communicating learning goals and processes to students, listening to understand and interpret student comments, questioning to get behind student thinking and scaffold student learning, and checking for understanding

**FIGURE 3.6**

Template for Team Planning

| Lesson: | |
|---|---|
| **Unit Goal and Essential Question (if prepared):** | |
| **Daily Learning Target(s):** | |
| **Focus Question(s):** | |
| **Response Structure(s):** | |

| Expected Responses | Follow-Up Questions |
|---|---|
| **Acceptable response(s):** | Questions to extend the learning of students who are already proficient: |
| **Possible misconception(s):** | Questions to scaffold thinking of students who have a misconception or make an error: |
| **Possible error(s):** | *How will we respond when some students do not learn?* |

to secure formative feedback and adjust the lesson to ensure it is in the "sweet spot" for most students. They also encourage student questions and build in pauses for student reflection to support self-regulation.

Shifting from teacher-directed, transmission-oriented instruction to student-owned, constructive learning requires students to understand the *what*, *why*, and *how* of a given lesson. Without a clear understanding of the learning destination, most students remain dependent on teachers.

During a facilitated lesson, the ratio of student-to-teacher talk increases. In this case, a major goal of the facilitator is to engage students in speaking and listening and to guide the focus of dialogue to extend learning for all. This requires a special kind of listening—what Wiliam (2011) refers to as interpretive listening—that involves seeking to understand the thinking behind an individual's words. Wiliam distinguishes this from evaluative listening, which focuses on evaluating statements for their correctness or the extent to which they align with one's own thinking.

Quality questioning is the hallmark of facilitation and encompasses the question types referenced earlier—focus questions, teacher-prepared follow-up questions, student questions, and emerging questions. Skilled facilitators bring questions to the classroom, pose focus questions to activate student thinking around learning targets, and adjust follow-up questions as needed to extend individual and group learning. They also make space for and actively invite student questions.

Student thinking and speaking that result from these questions provide a stream of formative feedback for teachers who, because they are listening interpretively, use student responses to make in-the-moment decisions about next instructional steps. This immediate calibration is a skill developed through intentional daily practice. The strategy outlined in Figure 3.7 supports development of this instructional practice.

**Set the stage for learning.** All formative lessons provide students with up-front structuring that affords the opportunity to internalize daily learning targets and obtain a basic understanding of how the class will proceed. This first step makes transparent the purpose and processes of the day's learning. This not only provides students with information enabling them to be partners in their learning but also serves to reduce anxiety by eliminating uncertainty. The following tasks are usually included in this portion of the lesson.

*Unpack daily learning targets and success criteria.* Understanding these two parts of a lesson design is essential to a student's ability to seek and use feedback that helps guide learning. Simply posting these elements on the

**FIGURE 3.7**

Components in Facilitation of a Formative Conversation

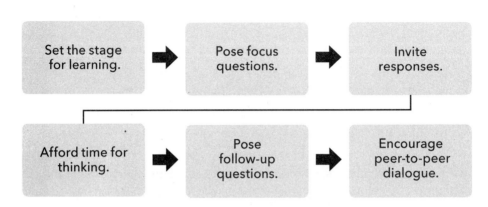

board is not adequate. Time must be allocated for students to make meaning of the statements. This can begin with partner dialogue, during which students identify questions they may have about terminology and translate the statements into their own words. The skilled teacher monitors these student conversations to ensure they all understand the direction in which the class is moving.

*Preview response structures and processes.* Structuring also involves orienting students to the ways in which they will be asked to participate in the day's learning. This includes a preview of the processes and protocols that will be used to structure their engagement. This does not mean the teacher provides step-by-step directions; rather, the teacher should offer students an overview of how they will be learning and the expectations for their engagement in class.

*Reinforce norms and mindsets.* Students will not assimilate the "new" norms emphasized in this book by hearing them once and never revisiting them. These norms, including think times, elimination of hand-raising, and learning from peers, run counter to long-established habits, many of which have been entrenched over years of schooling. Replacing traditional ways of thinking about appropriate school behavior is an important facet of building a new culture. Effective learning facilitators refocus student attention on these norms as each lesson begins.

**Pose focus questions.** Focus questions are springboards for formative lessons. Well-designed questions serve to center student attention on the learning targets for the day. They serve as hubs around which productive class dialogue occurs. Typically, two to four focus questions strategically placed throughout a lesson are sufficient to generate formative feedback to use when deciding on instructional next steps. The delivery or presentation of these questions affects student responses, so consider the value of the following strategies.

*Ask with interest in students' responses.* Dillon (1988) offers this simple piece of advice, noting that students too often assume that teachers are interested in their own answers rather than students' thinking. The tone and tenor used in the posing of a question can influence a student's reception of that question and subsequent response. Bracketing questions—that is, calling attention to their importance in a lesson—is important. This can be done with lead-in comments such as "The focus for our learning today is on this question . . ." or "Take a moment to think about this question as we begin today's lesson."

*Project on screen or write on board.* Spotlighting the written version of a prepared focus question helps learners decode and process the question. The written version augments the verbal delivery of the question to underscore its importance. This also scaffolds the use of think time 1 for both students and teacher.

*Afford extended think time 1 for individual student thinking.* The three- to five-second pause is often insufficient for student decoding of a complex question and retrieval of relevant knowledge from their long-term memories. Extended pauses help students jot down their initial thinking and offer their most thoughtful responses. These extended pauses can range from 15 seconds to a couple minutes, depending on the complexity of the question, the lesson goal, and the developmental level of students. The three- to five-second rule is appropriate for follow-up questions at lower levels of cognitive demand. On the other hand, longer pauses may be required when follow-up questions call for complex responses resulting from deeper thinking. This includes many questions at the analyze, create, and evaluate levels. Moreover, some students may require additional time. Teacher judgment is the best determinant of when to afford extra time to which students.

**Invite responses.** What if you replaced a volunteer's single response with a strategy to elicit responses from all class members? What might be the benefits? All-response systems enable this, and current technology extends possibilities. Most of us have experience with low-tech strategies such as signals (e.g., thumbs-up/down), work samples (e.g., small whiteboards), and choral responses. These work well with closed or short-answer questions, but they don't accommodate lengthier responses to higher-level questions. Today, we can choose from a wide range of apps and platforms to elicit all students' initial thinking about more complex focus questions. This opens up a range of possibilities for formative feedback to teachers, student responders, and their peers.

This is not to suggest that more traditional response formats are never appropriate. Holding all students accountable for forming an initial response is, however, an important first step in helping them use feedback. (Chapter 6 explores traditional and electronic options and provides guidelines for their selection and use.) The selection of the most appropriate response structures for a given lesson is a task associated with strategic lesson design.

*Signal for the oral sharing of response(s).* Whether you plan for students to respond orally or in writing via an all-response system, it is important to indicate who is to respond when. Callouts (i.e., when students answer aloud without being recognized) undermine student accountability and interfere with the clear reception of formative feedback. Adopting structures to counter this tendency is critical to effective classroom management. Consider the following possibilities:

- Many elementary teachers teach students to display a thumbs-up in the center of their chest when they are ready to respond. There are other signals that mean "I'm still thinking" and "I don't understand the question." After five seconds or so, the teacher names a student to respond.
- When using all-response systems, some teachers ask students to withhold the sharing of responses until they see (or hear) a signal for everyone to publicly display their responses.
- In the case of think-pair-share, teachers can instruct both partners to think until one is designated to speak. The teacher has students continue thinking until time is called—at which point partners are asked to speak.

These strategies promote multiple purposes. They (1) scaffold the use of think time 1 for all, (2) set the expectation that all students share their current thinking about a topic, and (3) discourage callouts.

*Monitor to ensure all students are responding.* During the enforced think time, it is important to move around and ensure that all students are preparing responses (e.g., by jotting down ideas or recording electronic responses) or responding as indicated if in pairs or collaborative groups.

**Afford time for thinking.** The second pause, think time 2, is to ensure that all students and the teacher have an opportunity to reflect on the response(s). When one student answers aloud in a whole-class setting, the pause provides everyone with the chance to process and decide how to respond. In the case of response systems that enable all students to publicly display their answers, the pause needs to be long enough for the reading and processing of all responses.

*Have students compare their responses to others'.* Students know that the teacher may ask any one of them whether they agree or disagree with the speaker and why. This can be used as a form of self-feedback.

*Use the pause to decide on follow-up questions.* Use the extended think time to be deliberate in coming up with one or more appropriate follow-up questions.

**Pose follow-up questions.** If the speaking student chooses not to modify or extend his or her response, either the teacher or another student may pose a question to the speaker or the entire class.

*Use think time 2 for follow-up questions.* The pause should be used for all questions, not just focus questions. Remind students of this by using the pause yourself before naming a student to respond to others' comments.

**Encourage peer-to-peer dialogue.** We need to increase student-to-student talk and encourage students to offer dialogic feedback to one another. However, most students are unaccustomed to this practice and may be reticent to react to their peer's statements without prompting.

*Elicit student-to-student talk in whole-class settings.* Our usual tendency is to react to students' comments with statements of our own. Therefore, we need to explicitly communicate an expectation for peer interactions by engaging in moves designed to serve this end. Figure 3.8 identifies five such moves—along with relevant strategies.

*Activate selected response structure.* A range of response structures support peer-to-peer dialogue. Think-pair-share is the one that is most frequently used. Other collaborative structures that support this goal are detailed in Chapter 6. Productive dialogue within these small-group structures is more likely to occur in classrooms where teachers have scaffolded peer-to-peer interactions during whole-class discussion (using the moves detailed in Figure 3.8).

## Culture Builder

The third primary role of the teacher is one executed in partnership with students. It begins on the first day of class and occurs daily in an intentional manner. The goal is to create an environment in which each student feels valued, respected, safe, and capable—one in which all students assume a growth mindset and accept responsibility for their own learning.

**FIGURE 3.8**

Facilitating Student-to-Student Interactions During Whole-Class Discussion

| Teacher Move | Strategy | Anticipated Student Response |
|---|---|---|
| Encourage students to respond to one another's oral responses. *(This move encourages peer-to-peer feedback.)* | Provide think time 2 after a student comment. Then invite peer comments by asking, for example, "What is your response to _____'s comment? Do you agree or disagree? Do you have a question?" | Students listen actively to their peer's response and (1) agree and add to the comment, (2) ask a question to the speaker, or (3) disagree and provide evidence for a different response. |
| Invite students to offer a different point of view from the one provided by the speaker. *(This variation on the previous move is particularly appropriate during a discussion in which multiple perspectives are likely to emerge.)* | Paraphrase a speaker's response. Then ask all class members to signal agreement or disagreement. Name a student who signaled a counter position to offer his or her perspective. | Students compare the speaker's point of view to their own. They provide evidence for differing perspectives or offer support for their agreement. |
| Invite students to pose a question to a peer who has just offered a "provocative" response. *(This move differs from the first in that the request is for a question— not for agreement or disagreement.)* | Following a student comment, ask others, "What questions do you have for _____?" Afford all students time to think about a student's comment and form a question for that student. Then name a student to pose his or her question. | All students reflect on the speaker's comment and form a question. Students may use stems and prompts as they prepare their questions. |
| Pose a "wondering" of your own about a student's response, and ask other students to respond. | Listen to identify a portion of the speaker's comment that might promote curiosity. Pose a question and ask the entire class to think and be ready for a response. For example, you might say, "_____'s comment causes me to wonder _____. How would others of you respond to my question?" | All students use think time 1 after your question. A volunteer is invited to lead off. Other students are expected to offer their reactions, adding to one another's ideas or offering new ones. |

| Teacher Move | Strategy | Anticipated Student Response |
|---|---|---|
| Pose a question that lends itself to multiple points of view, and invite students to "take a stand." | Pose a question and invite students to select one of several different responses. Afford them a way to signal their responses and open up the floor for discussion. (Note: Some teachers use a "four corners" strategy and have students move to a specified place in the room to signal their responses. They provide time for those who chose the same response to share views before opening up whole-class discussion.) | Students listen to the question and decide which position they want to take. They prepare a rationale for their selected perspective. When called upon, they share and compare their perspectives with classmates, adding to others' comments, challenging different points of view, and posing questions to better understand other perspectives. |

What are the characteristics of such a learning culture, and what can teachers do to cocreate such a culture with their students? There are countless ways of describing this culture, but four attributes stand out in classrooms where questioning is used for formative feedback. They are collaborative, open, respectful, and equitable—a CORE culture (Walsh, 2016).

Think of culture either as a way of being together in a classroom or as the way class members approach the business of learning. Cultures spring from both norms (shared beliefs about how to behave and interact) and structures (the ways in which activities are arranged or organized). Each of the four identified attributes can be strengthened through the intentional use of strategic norms and structures.

**Collaborative classroom.** Dialogue is a collaborative—not an individual—activity, requiring two or more individuals to work together to achieve a common goal. Dialogic feedback involves multiple parties jointly constructing a conversation that produces information everyone can use to advance their learning. In a collaborative classroom, this includes both teacher-to-student and student-to-student interactions. When this occurs, students value collaboration more than competition, a traditional feature of classrooms reinforced by grading practices (National Academies of Sciences, Engineering, and Medicine, 2018). To advance a collaborative way of thinking, teachers must be intentional in communicating expectations and selecting appropriate structures.

# Classroom Artifact

## Building a Safe, Comfortable Environment for Reciprocal Feedback

Social-emotional learning is important for all students, but it is essential for middle school students. Jane Haithcock, an 8th grade ELA teacher at Liberty Middle School, is acutely aware of this and plans her lessons with this as an important backdrop. She believes it important that she and her students coconstruct a class culture in which every student feels fully accepted and where mistakes are seen as opportunities for learning. She reinforces these norms in a lesson designed to prepare students for *The Outsiders* by S.E. Hinton. One of the questions to which students respond as they rotate through a "speed dating" lineup is *When have you felt like an outsider?* As they exchange responses, they continue building respect for diversity, one of the hallmarks of Mrs. Haithcock's classroom.

*Set a norm for collaboration.* Norms can evolve from expectations that are clearly communicated and reinforced. In the case of collaboration, begin by encouraging students to think and talk about why it is important to support one another as they learn. Students can share ways in which they are comfortable supporting others and how they like to receive help. Norms can be expressed through clear and succinct statements that are posted publicly. An example of such an expectation is *When we work and learn together, everyone benefits.*

*Select collaborative response structures to reinforce the norm.* Emphasis has been placed on the importance of strategically selected response structures. Reliance on hand-raisers to answer questions reinforces a competitive, individualistic norm associated with traditional schooling. By contrast, use of collaborative structures reinforces the norm of collaboration and scaffolds the emergence of a classroom learning community.

**Open classroom.** Openness conveys a nonjudgmental position—a willingness to listen to understand different perspectives and seemingly incorrect responses. It stems from an acknowledgment that individuals are at different places on their learning journey and possess different experiences and background knowledge. I do not mean that all questions should be open-ended or that there are no incorrect answers. Rather, this norm is based on the notion that in a learning community, everyone should feel comfortable speaking even when they are uncertain of the correctness of their position. A sample expression of this norm is *Mistakes provide opportunities for learning.* Teachers who effectively use questions for formative assessment emphasize psychological safety and risk-taking and seek to nurture student self-confidence to the level that learners feel safe making mistakes (Organization for Economic Co-Operation and Development, 2005).

*Challenge the "right answer" approach to learning.* Students need opportunities to consider the ways in which they can learn from mistakes and errors and to appreciate their own and their classmates' struggles. This norm supports positive social-emotional development, helping to eliminate personal embarrassment and deter students from making fun of peers who are experiencing difficulties in learning.

*Provide opportunities for students to appreciate different approaches and to learn from mistakes.* Many teachers use wrong answers as teaching tools, selecting an incorrect answer to analyze as a whole class, thereby giving students an opportunity to think through a faulty line of reasoning. In a Teaching Channel video that has gone viral, math teacher Leah Alcala demonstrates this strategy (https://learn.teachingchannel.com/video/class-warm-up-routine).

**Respectful classroom.** Respectfulness is an active expression and extension of openness. Put simply, openness will not take root without respect for individuals and their comments. Trust, a primary facilitator of dialogic feedback (Carless, 2013), is also an outgrowth of respectful relationships. When teacher–student and student–student relationships are grounded in respect, all members of the classroom community come to believe they can count on one another for support. Risk-taking then occurs without fear of ridicule or embarrassment. This is another cornerstone of a culture that nurtures questioning, dialogue, and feedback.

*Explicitly teach students the importance of listening to and respecting others' contributions to the class.* Many elementary teachers teach their students to preface their comments to peers with one of these two statements: "I respectfully agree with you and would like to add . . . ." "I respectfully disagree with you because . . . ." Teachers of older students may want to suggest alternative statements, such as "I appreciate what you are saying. I have a different perspective." The important thing is to have conversations with students about the importance of listening appreciatively to others and responding in a thoughtful manner.

**Equitable classroom.** When equitable participation is valued as important to a formative classroom environment, we see two distinct results. First, when students are included, they feel valued. Second, when collaborative structures scaffold participation by all, students come to value different perspectives and learn the value of hearing all voices. Equity promotes inclusivity and opportunities for everyone to learn. Equally important is the role equity plays in providing teachers with formative feedback that is balanced and representative of the progress of the class as a whole. Without balanced feedback, teachers cannot create a "sweet spot" for learning that promotes engagement of all. The following classroom norms underpin an equitable classroom: *Learn with and from one another, listening to understand all perspectives and encouraging peers who are not speaking to express their ideas. Monitor your own speaking to ensure you participate in but do not dominate class discussion.*

Collaboration, openness, respect, and equity are interdependent. They work together to create a culture in which students feel comfortable and confident using questioning, dialogue, and feedback to progress toward identified learning outcomes. As teachers, we cannot by ourselves create classroom cultures infused with these four traits. We can, however, explicitly teach associated expectations, model them as we interact with students, select structures that scaffold, reinforce expectations, and celebrate behaviors that exhibit these values.

## *Classroom Artifact*
### Three Teacher Roles in Practice

Courtney Evans, 7th grade mathematics teacher at Oxford Middle School, exemplifies the three teacher roles spotlighted in this chapter: lesson designer, learning facilitator, and culture builder. During the 2020-21 school year, Courtney—like all teachers—was challenged by the events and circumstances of COVID-19. Faced with a hybrid schedule, masking, and social distancing, Courtney committed to designing and facilitating lessons that engaged students academically as well as socially and emotionally.

She made use of quality questioning practices as she offered her students multiple entry points for engagement during face-to-face lessons despite the challenges presented by the physical modifications.

 In the middle of the year, one class was organized around this focus question: *How can the properties of equality help me generate equivalent expressions?* Over the course of a lesson, Courtney seamlessly moved students through a series of learning strategies that culminated in their creation of success criteria for written responses to problems. Among the response structures she used were think-pair-share, display of work products on dry-erase boards, public sharing of responses on Nearpod, and whole-class dialogue. Throughout the class, Courtney modeled skills and dispositions she expected of her students and used their responses as feedback to help her confirm next instructional moves. This lesson provides a look inside a formative classroom where teachers and students assume important roles and responsibilities.

## Feedforward

Teacher design and facilitation of daily lessons provide the stage and setting for student assumption of roles and responsibilities that lead to success in learning. Cocreation of a safe environment enhances the opportunity for everyone to engage actively in learning. Many students, however, do not arrive to our classrooms with the mindsets or skills required to discharge new roles and responsibilities. The next chapter makes these student capacities explicit and provides strategies and suggestions for use in nurturing and strengthening them in a classroom setting.

## Transferring Principles to Practice

Use Figure 3.9 to decide how you would like to incorporate the ideas presented in this chapter to plan for and support your students' ability to seek and use formative feedback. Identify practices you are currently using and would like to strengthen along with others you may wish to consider.

**FIGURE 3.9**

Transferring Principles to Practice: Teacher Beliefs, Roles, and Responsibilities

| Opportunities for Practice | Classroom Applications | |
| --- | --- | --- |
| | **Teacher Learning** | **Teacher Facilitation of Student Learning** |
| **Use the instructional core to reflect on relationships in your classroom.** | With members of your PLC, examine Figure 3.1. Talk about how you might use questioning and feedback to strengthen students' relationships with the content and one another. | Engage students in dialogue focused on the following questions: (1) What most supports you in making meaning of content? (2) In what ways does interacting with your classmates help you better understand and connect with the content you are studying? |
| **Reflect on the teacher roles and responsibilities in the formative classroom (Figure 3.3).** | Which of the three roles would you like to focus on more intentionally? How might you use resources in this chapter to enhance your performance in this area? | What type of information might you collect from your students to use as formative feedback to help you customize and prioritize behaviors associated with each of these roles? |
| **Use Figures 3.4 and 3.5 as you plan a lesson that incorporates questioning for formative feedback.** | If your team or PLC currently uses DuFour's four questions for planning, use Figure 3.5 to identify the suggested design tasks you currently incorporate into team planning. How might you use resources in this book to strengthen collaborative planning? | Reflect on one identified lesson to identify the ratio of students who mastered the daily learning targets to those who had not yet mastered them by the end of class. How did questioning assist in the collection of evidence to support this conclusion? How might you use questioning to frame next steps? |
| **Assess your confidence and competence as a facilitator of formative lessons (Figure 3.7).** | In which, if any, of the six identified areas do you believe yourself to be highly competent? What is your evidence? In which of these areas would you like to focus for improvement? Jot down one or two improvement goals to which you will commit. | Use the "anticipated student response" column of Figure 3.8 to assess the interactive skills/behaviors of a selected class. In which of these areas do your students currently perform at a relatively high level? In which would you like to work with them toward improvement? How might you proceed? |

| Opportunities for Practice | Classroom Applications | |
| --- | --- | --- |
| | Teacher Learning | Teacher Facilitation of Student Learning |
| **What is your reaction to the concept of a CORE culture?** To what extent does your understanding of the four components align with that presented in this book? | Talk with members of your collaborative team about the concept of a CORE culture. Think about the extent to which your school's values reinforce each of the features of this culture. What are the advantages of working across the school to create this type of culture? | Select a group of students. Create two or three questions to assess their understanding and agreement with the four components of a CORE culture. |

# Skills and Dispositions That Empower Learners

---

*What specific skills and dispositions do students need to master if they are to participate actively in quality questioning, dialogue, and feedback?*

---

Empowering learners involves the development of discrete skills and dispositions that equip them to become seekers, users, and generators of feedback. Success in teaching these skills depends on renorming—changing the way students think about how to act and interact in the classroom community.

One challenge for teachers is determining how to support individuals and an entire class as they move from a reliance on old beliefs and habits to an acceptance of new norms and behaviors. Imagine the following shifts associated with a student's journey toward a new way of being and behaving as a learner. The skills and dispositions outlined in this chapter facilitate and reinforce these shifts:

- **From guessing to grappling.** Many students are conditioned to guess the teacher's intended answer. They become frustrated when asked to work through problems and concepts themselves. Grappling requires persistence, or the willingness to stick with a learning task. When students grapple, they generate and use self-feedback and identify specific areas of misunderstanding and confusion that enable them to seek targeted feedback from others.
- **From surface-level understanding to deep learning.** This transition is key to the first. Guesses are easier to make when learning occurs at the surface level. Deep learning, however, involves peeling back possible misconceptions and making new connections. Grappling is often necessary during this process.

- **From reaction to reflection.** Reflection involves pausing and rethinking—versus reaction, which can be simply defined as "speaking without thinking" and is frequently evaluative, interferes with listening to understand, and shuts down productive dialogue. By contrast, giving and receiving feedback depend on a reflective stance.
- **From interrogation to inquiry.** The purpose behind questioning is important. Interrogation often leads to confrontation, and inquiry typically leads to collaboration. Dialogue depends on collaborative thinking. Unfortunately, this is not the usual model that students see or hear in most classrooms (or society).
- **From competition to collaboration.** Collaboration is one of the hallmarks of a CORE culture. It underlies dialogic feedback and supports its use, whereas competition undermines these.

# Student Roles and Responsibilities

Defining and clarifying students' various roles and responsibilities is essential if they are to take control of their learning. Viewing these through the lens of quality questioning, dialogue, and feedback is necessary to identify and develop the skills and dispositions that support formative processes. When this is done, three significant roles and associated responsibilities emerge (see Figure 4.1). Interestingly, each connects to specific teacher roles and responsibilities (as outlined in Chapter 3).

## Student as Self-Assessor

Students' ability to seek and provide feedback is contingent on their ability to self-assess—to compare their current knowledge and skills to those embedded in a learning target. Self-assessment also encompasses an appraisal of one's ability to identify and use the cognitive strategies needed to attain a given learning target (Bailey & Heritage, 2018). When students view themselves as assessors of their own learning, they can then provide others with accurate feedback about their current understanding or performance and use feedback provided by teachers and peers to reflect and self-correct. Skilled self-assessors draw on metacognitive skills to carry out four key related responsibilities.

**They use learning targets as a GPS to guide and monitor learning.** Self-assessment depends on learners' understanding of the purpose and substance of learning outcomes. Successful self-assessors focus on and make meaning of daily learning targets and refer to them throughout a lesson. They use these as benchmarks to measure progress in learning.

*Connection to teacher roles and responsibilities*: Lesson designers create daily learning targets. Learning facilitators offer time and support for unpacking daily learning targets and related success criteria.

**They ask questions of themselves to identify possible gaps in learning.** A core skill of self-assessment is the ability to compare one's current level of knowledge and skill proficiency to that identified in a learning target. Successful learners engage in this metacognitive activity throughout a lesson and silently and routinely generate and answer questions to achieve this end.

**FIGURE 4.1**

Student Roles and Responsibilities in a Formative Classroom

- Use learning targets as a GPS to guide and monitor learning.
- Ask self-questions.
- Use others' questions as catalysts for self-assessment.
- Form and ask questions aloud to request feedback from others.

**Self-Assessor**

- Use questions to make new connections.
- Proactively seek feedback.
- Make meaning of feedback.
- Use feedback to affirm, correct, or extend knowledge.

**Knowledge Constructor**

- Provide honest responses to questions.
- Actively listen during class dialogue.
- Provide feedback to peers.
- Engage in collaborative thinking and speaking.

**Collaborative Contributor**

*Connection to teacher roles and responsibilities*: Learning facilitators provide routine pauses (think times 1 and 2) and reinforce student use of the silence to reflect on progress toward an identified learning target.

**They use others' questions as catalysts for thinking and self-assessment.** Skilled self-assessors know that other people's questions are tools for self-assessment. This is true of all classroom questions—those posed by teachers, posed by peers, directed to oneself, and directed to others. Students who assume this responsibility listen actively to every question, use think time 1 to decode the question and form a response, listen actively to responses, and use think time 2 to make meaning of others' responses and compare them to their own.

*Connection to teacher roles and responsibilities*: Lesson designers create focus questions meant to promote student thinking and knowledge retrieval that enable self-assessment. Learning facilitators use think times 1 and 2 to provide opportunities for student thinking and self-assessment.

**They form and ask questions to address discrepancies between their own thinking and ideas expressed by others.** Self-assessors are cued into the external environment. They are alert to signals that confirm or challenge their own understanding. They form questions to get behind the thinking of those whose statements contradict their own thinking. They also seek clarification and additional information from those with whom they agree.

*Connection to teacher roles and responsibilities*: Learning facilitators engage students in formative conversations, generating dialogue that yields formative feedback for all learners. They also emphasize the importance of using pauses to form and pose questions that clarify others' thinking and their own understanding.

## Classroom Artifact

### Structured Opportunities for Peer Feedback During a Socratic Seminar

Samantha Hammond has a vision for her students. She wants them to interact in a culture founded on trust and respect to make real-world connections as they listen and learn from one another. To this end, she scaffolds student development of critical skills over the course of the year. She introduces norms and expectations and explicitly teaches and reviews them. She creates anchor charts containing sentence starters, models think times and question-asking, works on changing her own mindset related to control, and is intentional in helping her students assume responsibilities as she gradually releases control.

As the school year ends, Ms. Hammond engages her students in a Socratic seminar to delve into the novel they are reading. She makes each listener (seated in the outside circle) responsible for documenting the skills used by one assigned peer who is participating in the discussion (seated in the inner circle). At the conclusion of each round, partners provide each other with feedback about their use of cognitive and social skills.

## Student as Knowledge Constructor

Developing a clear, complete, and accurate understanding of content is the desired outcome of formative feedback. Questioning and dialogue support students in the use of feedback to accomplish this end. Learners are therefore motivated to engage in these two practices when they recognize that no one can "give" them knowledge—that they are responsible for engaging in the cognitive processes that support construction of their own understanding. Skilled knowledge constructors draw on metacognitive skills to carry out four key related responsibilities.

**They use questions to make new connections.** Hattie and Clarke (2019) note that questions to activate prior knowledge and experiences are vastly underused in most classrooms. Learners who understand their role as knowledge constructors value and use questions to bring prior knowledge to the forefront—both to test it for accuracy and, if valid, to connect it to new facts and skills.

*Connection to teacher roles and responsibilities*: Lesson designers create questions to activate prior knowledge and understanding. Learning facilitators pose these questions at the beginning of a lesson to help students tap into their long-term memories and retrieve relevant knowledge and experiences.

**They proactively seek feedback to address identified needs.** A significant amount of research focuses on students' help-seeking behaviors. For example, Hattie's (2008) review of variables that affect student achievement reveals this behavior to have a high effect size ($d = 0.72$). The most accessible tool for seeking help is question-asking. Chapter 5 addresses strategies teachers can use to nurture all types of student questions.

*Connection to teacher roles and responsibilities*: Learning facilitators encourage students to pose questions when they are confused or need assistance. They also develop student skills in question-asking.

**They make meaning of feedback and connect this to current thinking.** Meaning-making and connection-making are important cognitive skills, both of which are required for students to use feedback from others. To be effective, external feedback must "ultimately trigger inner dialogue in students' minds" around the focus of the learning (Nicol, 2010, p. 504). This involves students in actively decoding feedback information and internalizing it. Active listening is a prerequisite to this, but listening cannot be assumed. It must be taught through modeling and direct instruction. Students demonstrate they are actively listening by

- Using silence after a classmate stops speaking to think about what the speaker said and to compare the speaker's thinking to their own.
- Asking questions to better understand a speaker's point of view.
- Waiting before adding their own ideas to ensure the speaker has completed his or her thoughts.
- Accurately paraphrasing what another student says.
- Looking at the speaker and giving nonverbal cues they are paying attention.

*Connection to teacher roles and responsibilities*: Lesson designers prepare to provide meaningful feedback to all learners. Learning facilitators underscore the importance of interpretive listening and use pauses to process students' comments, which are then used to prepare feedback.

**They use feedback to affirm, revise, or extend knowledge and skills.** This is a complex metacognitive task enabled by the previous actions (i.e., meaning-making and connection-making). Use of external feedback also depends on three learner attributes: (1) openness to another's suggestions, (2) an ability to assess the potential value of this information to continued learning, and (3) a willingness to act on the feedback provided (Bailey & Heritage, 2018). When students meet these three criteria and use feedback, they compare and contrast their current thinking to that offered by their teacher or classmates to determine the extent of alignment (or misalignment). This is a high-impact strategy employed by teachers during direct instruction (Marzano, 2017). Bailey and Heritage (2018) emphasize the connection between self-assessment and use of external feedback, writing "Not all feedback may be useful; students need to know this and learn to discriminate among the feedback comments they receive" (p. 35).

*Connection to teacher roles and responsibilities*: Learning facilitators are intentional and explicit in teaching and modeling the use of feedback to modify or extend their thinking and knowledge. They do this through the use of formative conversations, which help students reflect on and revise their own thinking.

## Student as Collaborative Contributor

This role is the gateway to a classroom learning community in which students learn with and from one another. Students who discharge related responsibilities understand the importance of collaborative thinking. They listen to and value their peers' comments, and they are comfortable and accountable in sharing their own thinking and insights. Skilled collaborative contributors draw on metacognitive skills to carry out four key related responsibilities.

**They provide honest responses to questions to let others know their level of understanding.** This student mindset cannot be overemphasized. By openly sharing their current thinking, students enable teachers to offer helpful feedback. They also contribute to peer learning through both correct and incorrect responses. When students embrace the norm related to learning from errors, they appreciate classmates' responses as catalysts for reflecting on their own thinking. In a CORE (collaborative, open, respectful, equitable) culture, peers react to one another's responses with corrective and affirming feedback as they engage in dialogue.

*Connection to teacher roles and responsibilities*: Culture builders reinforce the norm of students responding even when they are not certain of the correctness of their thinking. They use structures to promote collaboration. Learning facilitators scaffold peer-to-peer interactions and seek to increase the ratio of student talk to their own.

**They actively listen to others during class dialogue.** Hattie (2012) argues that "the most important job of teachers is to listen" (p. 73). Most of us would agree this is also true for students. Listening is key to learning—both in and out of school—yet students are rarely provided instruction in *how* to listen.

*Connection to teacher roles and responsibilities*: Learning facilitators underscore the connection between the use of think time and active listening.

They also incorporate facilitation strategies that build accountability for listening and responding to peers.

**They provide honest feedback and ask questions to peers.** Peer-to-peer interactions are powerful sources of feedback when students view them as such. This involves shifting the thinking of those students who believe teachers are the source of all knowledge in the classroom. A CORE culture emphasizes the importance of respect for peers' thinking and opens up possibilities for students to learn from one another. It also encourages individual students to openly agree and disagree with one another and to pose questions that clarify the thinking of those who may have different perspectives. Peer feedback is potentially the most powerful of all feedback. This is attributable to both the learner's ability to understand the language used by a classmate and the proximity both students have to the learning and their experiences (Bailey & Heritage, 2018).

*Connection to teacher roles and responsibilities*: Learning facilitators underscore the connection between the use of think time and active listening. They also incorporate facilitation strategies that build accountability for listening and responding to peers.

**They engage in collaborative thinking and speaking to build a collective understanding.** Dialogue is a powerful way for students to deepen knowledge and understanding through the intentional use of collaborative thinking and speaking. The process involves a give and take, during which students offer ideas, receive feedback from others, and develop an expanded understanding of content. We can compare a dialogical classroom to a research laboratory in which individuals are generating and testing ideas, drawing on one another's strengths and insights.

*Connection to teacher roles and responsibilities*: Culture builders create an environment in which collaborative thinking and speaking thrive. Learning facilitators provide the structures and model the norms that nurture and reinforce learning in a collaborative community.

## Skills Associated with Seeking and Using Formative Feedback

Students who are active participants in a formative classroom draw on a set of core skills that span these three roles and related responsibilities (Figure 4.2). Four categories of skills—metacognitive, cognitive, use-of-knowledge, and social—serve as the broad organizers. Each is composed of three skill subsets,

**FIGURE 4.2**

Compendium of Skills Associated with Questioning for Formative Feedback

| Metacognitive Skills | | |
| --- | --- | --- |
| **Self-Questioning** | **Self-Monitoring** | **Self-Correcting** |
| • Question yourself to assess initial understanding of a learning target.<br>• Ask questions to monitor your progress toward a learning target.<br>• Question yourself to make meaning of feedback. | • Identify the gap between your current knowledge or skill level and the identified learning target.<br>• Compare your current thinking to that expressed by others.<br>• Assess your progress toward a learning target. | • Use feedback to identify misconceptions or errors.<br>• Apply information obtained through feedback to identified errors and adjust your response.<br>• Respond to questions intended to build correct or expanded understanding. |
| **Cognitive Skills** | | |
| **Meaning-Making** | **Connection-Making** | **Question-Asking** |
| • Translate other people's comments into your own words.<br>• Relate others' comments to your knowledge and experiences.<br>• Integrate new information into your schema. | • Use questions to connect to and retrieve information from long-term memory.<br>• Link feedback from the teacher or classmates to what you currently think about the subject.<br>• Identify similarities and differences between your ideas and those of others. | • Ask questions to clarify when you do not understand or are confused.<br>• Pose questions to better understand feedback offered by your teacher or classmates.<br>• Ask questions to clarify the thinking of a classmate to whom you are giving feedback. |

## Use-of-Knowledge Skills

| Surface | Deep/Transfer | Metacognitive |
|---|---|---|
| • Clarify facts or procedures required to build initial understanding.<br>• Test the accuracy of your tacit knowledge.<br>• Use task-level feedback to correct mistakes and errors. | • Clarify your understanding of the relationship between a new concept and ideas in your existing knowledge base.<br>• Use process-level feedback to reflect on current conceptual understanding and test its accuracy.<br>• Use dialogic feedback to extend your understanding of the relationships between different ideas. | • Use teacher modeling of metacognitive processing to reflect on your own approach.<br>• Identify voids and errors in your metacognitive thinking.<br>• Modify and extend your current approach to thinking about and monitoring learning based on feedback from teachers and peers. |

## Social Skills

| Speaking | Listening | Collaborating |
|---|---|---|
| • Speak clearly and loudly enough so everyone can hear.<br>• Speak to classmates and the teacher.<br>• Speak at length to make your thinking visible to others. | • Look at the speaker and give nonverbal cues that you are paying attention.<br>• Use silence after a question is posed to decode (i.e., think about what the question is asking) and form an initial response.<br>• Use the pause following your teacher or a classmate's response to think about and interpret what was said. | • Use feedback from others to think about and confirm, revise, or extend your thinking.<br>• Offer feedback to classmates in a respectful manner when invited to do so.<br>• Respond to teachers' and classmates' questions about your thinking in a nondefensive manner. |

which are expressed as observable, documentable behaviors that can be taught and reinforced as part of ongoing instruction.

## Metacognitive Skills

This category of skills relates directly to the role of self-assessor. These are internal processing skills in which learners silently engage as they monitor and manage their progress toward identified learning outcomes. Self-questioning skills support other skills in this category, enabling students to self-monitor and self-correct. Explicit teaching of these skills helps learners understand the importance of their role as self-assessor. Associated prompts and stems scaffold student use of the skills (Figure 4.3).

## Cognitive Skills

These skills support students in the role of knowledge constructor. They involve the *how* of learning—the manner in which individuals receive, process, and store information. Two of the skill subsets—meaning-making and connection-making—relate to cognitive processing and storage of information. The third, question-asking, supports the other two. The first two are typically done silently or via scaffolding by another. Question-asking, however, is a public activity initiated by the learner. This may be an unfamiliar role to many students. The prompts and stems provided in Figure 4.4 can nurture and support them in this endeavor.

## Use-of-Knowledge Skills

This set of skills, which also supports the role of knowledge constructor—develops student understanding of different levels of knowledge. If students are to seek meaningful feedback at different stages of their learning, they need to understand the difference between surface and deep knowledge and how to seek assistance related to development of proficiency for each. Figure 4.5 offers skills and prompts for use in building surface knowledge, and Figure 4.6 provides a similar tool for use by students in deepening knowledge and understanding.

## FIGURE 4.3

Prompts to Support Self-Questioning Skills

| Skill | Sample Prompts and Stems |
|---|---|
| Question yourself to assess initial understanding of a learning target. | • How would I define the academic vocabulary embedded in the learning target?<br>• What, if anything, don't I understand about the target?<br>• How would I explain this target in my own words? |
| Ask questions to monitor your progress toward a learning target. | • Where am I in my progress toward attainment of the learning target?<br>• What is my evidence?<br>• What strategies can I use to progress toward proficiency? |
| Question yourself to make meaning of feedback. | • What does the feedback statement mean to me? How do I interpret the statement?<br>• How does the feedback relate to my current level of understanding or performance?<br>• What, specifically, can I do to correct or extend my knowledge or skills? |

## Classroom Artifact

### Strategic Use of Small-Group Structures
### Scaffolds Social Skills for Young Learners

Teachers at Athens Elementary School strategically use pairs and quads to organize their students for dialogue. Like many teachers, they carefully pair students and designate one as the "peanut butter" partner and the other as the "jelly" partner. These teachers then determine how best to pair these duos to form quads, which they call "sandwich" partners. With these building blocks in place, they can seamlessly move their students from the whole group to pairs to quads, depending on their purpose. In this video, we go inside a 3rd and 4th grade classroom and hear teachers reflect on the value of these small-group structures to the development of students' social skills and to their learning.

**FIGURE 4.4**

Prompts and Stems to Support Question-Asking Skills

| Skill | Sample Prompts and Stems |
|---|---|
| Ask questions to clarify when you do not understand or are confused. | • What do you mean when you say ____?<br>• Can you provide an example of ____?<br>• I'm not following you. Can you help me understand your thinking? |
| Pose questions to better understand feedback offered by your teacher or classmates. | • Would you restate this using different words?<br>• To what part of my response (or thinking) does your feedback relate? |
| Ask questions to clarify the thinking of a classmate to whom you are giving feedback. | • I heard you say ____. Is this correct?<br>• Can you say more about that?<br>• What makes you say that? |

**FIGURE 4.5**

Skills and Stems to Support Surface Learning

| Skill | Use When | Sample Prompts and Stems |
|---|---|---|
| Clarify facts or procedures required to build initial understanding. | • You don't know the meaning of a word or phrase.<br>• You don't understand how two things connect to each other. | • I'm not following you. Can you say this another way?<br>• Can you give me an example of ____?<br>• How does ____ relate to ____? |
| Test the accuracy of your tacit knowledge.* | • When you think you understand an idea or know how to do something, but it's different from what you are hearing about in class.<br>• When your experience led you to believe one thing, but no one has mentioned it.<br>• When you have something to add that hasn't been mentioned in the text or by the teacher. | • I've been thinking ____. Can this also be true?<br>• When I did ____, this seemed to work for me. Can this be another way to do this?<br>• I learned ____ from ____. Is this also a way to think about (or do) this? |

| Skill | Use When | Sample Prompts and Stems |
|---|---|---|
| Use task-level feedback to correct mistakes and errors. | When the teacher or a peer tells you your answer is wrong. | • I'm not clear about this answer (or conclusion). Please explain it to me.<br>• This is why I thought ____. Help me understand why this is not true. |

*Teachers may need to define *tacit knowledge* to students and help them understand how it can support their classroom learning.

## FIGURE 4.6

Skills and Stems to Support Deep Learning

| Skill | Use When | Sample Prompts and Stems |
|---|---|---|
| Clarify your understanding of the relationship between a new concept and what you have already learned. | • You wonder how one thing is like (or different from) another.<br>• You wonder whether one thing might have caused another. | • How is ____ similar to ____?<br>• How is ____ different from ____?<br>• What do ____ and ____ have in common?<br>• What may have contributed to ____?<br>• What resulted from ____?<br>• What effect would that have?<br>• What might have caused this? |
| • Use process-level feedback to reflect on current conceptual understanding and test its accuracy. | • You are trying to understand at what point you made an error or left out a step.<br>• You are attempting to apply what you've heard to the way you have been thinking about the topic. | • This is the way I was thinking about ____. What step am I missing?<br>• I don't understand why this is the case. Can you explain it another way?<br>• Here's why I think ____. Does this make sense to you?<br>• I'm still not clear about how what you just said relates to what I've been thinking. Can you help me understand how ____ connects to ____? |

*(continued)*

**FIGURE 4.6–**(*continued*)

Skills and Stems to Support Deep Learning

| Skill | Use When | Sample Prompts and Stems |
|---|---|---|
| Use dialogic feedback to extend your understanding of the relationships between different ideas. | • Someone introduced an idea you've never thought of before.<br>• You wonder about how another idea or concept might connect to the topic under discussion.<br>• You're curious about how ____ might affect ____. | • What makes you say that?<br>• What are some other instances in which this might be true?<br>• What might be the relationship between ____ and ____?<br>• Imagine ____. What might happen if ____? |

## Social Skills

Speaking, listening, and collaborative thinking are all key to dialogic feedback and support the role of collaborative contributor. Most students do not come to classrooms with a history of interactive experiences, especially for the purposes of affirming, challenging, or extending classmates' thinking. The sample prompts and stems in Figure 4.7 offer students go-to openers for sharing and collaborative thinking, providing a sense of confidence to reticent participants. When all students have access to these stems, they can use them to signal their intent to share in an expected and respectful manner.

# Dispositions That Support Questioning for Formative Feedback

Skills help students execute certain cognitive operations. Dispositions prompt them to use those skills, activating the will or motivation to do so. A simple definition of *disposition* is the tendency to think or act in a particular way. Costa and Kallick (2014) suggest that thinking dispositions are "tendencies toward particular patterns of intellectual behavior" (p. 19). They cite the contributions of Paul Ennis to their premise "that the disposition must be exercised reflectively. In other words, given the appropriate conditions, dispositions are not automatic" (p. 19). This suggests the need to make students aware of the *what* and *why* behind their dispositions and to support the development of dispositions integral to formative experiences.

**FIGURE 4.7**

Stems and Prompts to Support Peer-to-Peer Interactions

| Skill | Use When | Sample Prompts and Stems |
|---|---|---|
| Add to a class-mate's responses (elaborate). | You agree with what a peer has said and have something to add. | • I'd like to piggyback and add ____.<br>• I agree with you about ____ and would like to add ____. |
| Disagree with what someone else has said. | You think differently about a topic or have a different answer. | • I respectfully disagree.<br>• I hear you saying ____, but I have a different idea. How do you react to ____? |
| Ask a clarifying question. | You want to better understand someone else's idea. | • What makes you say that?<br>• I don't understand. Would you explain your thinking?<br>• Can you give me an example of ____? |
| Encourage a nonparticipating peer to speak. | You want to include someone who is not participating. | • I'm wondering what you're thinking about this, [classmate's name].<br>• I've been talking a lot. I'm wondering what someone else thinks. |

Bailey and Heritage (2018) argue that an overriding disposition of students who effectively use feedback and self-regulatory skills is the belief that "they can learn how to learn" (p. 10). They associate this with a growth mindset and single out a willingness to persevere and to imagine new possibilities as important dispositions for students who seek and use feedback.

Figure 4.8 draws from these thought leaders and from the experiences of teachers who have worked with their students toward these goals. The 10 highlighted dispositions align with the four categories of skills identified in this chapter. This resource can be used with students to develop their awareness of the habits of mind that support them as learners.

# Feedforward

The three roles, related responsibilities, and associated dispositions spotlighted in this chapter contribute to effective student engagement. Think of these as a sort of job description for students—a resource for conveying what is required to be successful learners. Being explicit with students about these promotes more effective involvement in questioning, dialogue, and formative feedback. Teaching and reinforcing the roles, responsibilities, and dispositions builds students' skill and will to participate confidently.

The quality of a given lesson affects the thrill of learning. Designing formative experiences is the focus of the next two chapters, which are intended to serve as an instruction manual of sorts for formulating powerful questions and selecting strategic response structures.

**FIGURE 4.8**

Dispositions Associated with Identified Skills

| Disposition | Evidence of Student Use |
| --- | --- |
| **Metacognitive** | |
| *Reflectiveness* | Students look back on prior thinking or behavior and learn from it. They look ahead to next steps to move their learning forward. |
| *Self-regulation* | Students can monitor their performance, identify deficits in thinking or performance (based on success criteria), and select strategies to move forward. |
| **Cognitive** | |
| *Perseverance/Persistence* | Students do not give up when confronting a difficult task; rather, they redouble their efforts, "stay the course," sustain individual efforts, and seek help as needed. |
| *Willingness to take reasonable risks* | Students are willing to move beyond the bounds of certainty to offer their current thinking. They understand that we all learn from our mistakes. |
| *Flexibility in thinking* | Students are willing to "try out" different types of thinking and points of view. They are open to feedback from others. |
| **Use-of-Knowledge** | |
| *Accuracy* | Students are motivated to reach a correct understanding. They reflect on their thinking to self-assess and self-correct. |
| *Application of prior knowledge to new situations* | Students activate prior knowledge and experiences and test their accuracy and relevance as they approach new learning. |

| Disposition | Evidence of Student Use |
|---|---|
| **Social** | |
| *Active listening* | Students listen to make meaning of others' comments. They look at a speaker with interest, think about what the speaker is saying, and ask questions to clarify what they may not, at first, understand. |
| *Open-mindedness* | Students are open to both positive and constructive feedback and to different perspectives. |
| *Ability to manage impulsivity* | Students think before speaking—whether receiving or giving feedback. They respond to comments by seeking to understand the underlying thinking. |

## Transferring Principles to Practice

Use Figure 4.9 to reflect on your students' current capacity to engage in questioning, dialogue, and feedback. Identify priorities for students in your schools.

**FIGURE 4.9**

Transferring Principles to Practice: Student Skills and Dispositions

| Opportunities for Practice | Classroom Applications | |
|---|---|---|
| | **Teacher Learning** | **Teacher Facilitation of Student Learning** |
| **Reflect on the six shifts in student thinking.** | With members of your collaborative team or PLC, reflect and engage in dialogue focused on the six proposed shifts in student thinking. Do they make sense to you? To what extent might your students benefit from thinking about these shifts? | Present the six proposed shifts to your students. Ask them to silently reflect on the list and assess their current ways of being in the classroom. You may wish to create a continuum for students to use in this activity. Following time for reflection, invite students to engage in dialogue and identify strengths and areas for growth. |

*(continued)*

**FIGURE 4.9–**(*continued*)

Transferring Principles to Practice: Student Skills and Dispositions

| Opportunities for Practice | Classroom Applications | |
| --- | --- | --- |
| | **Teacher Learning** | **Teacher Facilitation of Student Learning** |
| **Examine the three identified roles and related responsibilities for students (Figure 4.1).** | How might you use this framework to engage students in thinking and dialogue about their roles and responsibilities in questioning and formative feedback? | Plan a series of mini-lessons to introduce students to the roles and responsibilities in the formative classroom. Plan to address one role per lesson. |
| **Analyze the compendium of skills for students (Figure 4.2).** | Identify ways in which you might use this blueprint in planning and reflection related to student capacity to engage productively in questioning and formative feedback. | Review the compendium with students, focusing on the four broad categories and three subsets of skills. Help students understand the *what* and *why* of each category. |
| **Review the tools presented in Figures 4.3–4.7.** | Decide which tools best meet the needs of your students, given their grade level and your subject area. Think about how and when you might introduce the selected tools to your students. Modify the wording for skills and prompts as appropriate for your grade level and content area. | Reproduce selected tools for each student to have as accessible resources. Introduce each tool and give students an opportunity to immediately use the tool in an appropriate portion of the lesson. |
| **Consider how developing student awareness of identified dispositions might promote more effective engagement.** | With your team members, review Figure 4.8 to identify dispositions you would most value for your students, given their developmental levels. Talk about how you might present the concept of *disposition* to students, along with the specific dispositions you identify as having particular relevance in your classroom. | Engage students in dialogue about dispositions, what they are, and how they function to support learning. Present a limited number of dispositions and seek to support their development in daily lessons. |

# *Part* III

# Designing Formative Experiences

Questioning that results in dialogic feedback does not occur by accident; rather, it results from intentional and strategic teacher design of formative lessons and learning environments. Formative lesson design, best accomplished in collaboration with colleagues, is integrated into daily lesson planning and includes two primary focus areas: (1) questions to activate student thinking and responding and (2) structures intended to optimize the number of students who communicate their responses. The design of formative learning environments occurs over time in collaboration with students. Such environments are grounded in trusting relationships that underpin psychological safety. As explored so far in this book, they reflect shared beliefs about the purposes of questions, the primacy of learning for every student, and the valuing of time for thinking and processing others' responses.

Chapter 5 illuminates the characteristics of questions that generate student thinking about where they are in learning related to daily learning targets. Differentiated focus questions are the springboard for thinking and feedback that drive a lesson. Beyond the limited number of focus questions designed to activate initial student thinking, teacher designers anticipate probable misconceptions and other errors that may emerge and are prepared to pose follow-up questions to sustain student thinking and scaffold new understandings. Other questions emerge during a lesson depending on student responses.

Student questions can play a significant role in advancing dialogue and feedback. Three types of student questions are important to the process: metacognitive, academic, and dialogic questions. Each contributes in a specific and unique manner to students' capacity to seek, use, and provide feedback that can advance individual and collective learning.

Keep in mind that the goal of a well-designed focus question can be subverted if only a few student volunteers offer a response. Nevertheless, in most contemporary classrooms, a minority of students answer a majority of teacher questions. Although these students may get the right answers on the floor, teachers are left with an incomplete understanding of where all students are in their learning. With this in mind, Chapter 6 offers guidance in matching different contexts and question types to specific response structures and systems. The intent of these structures is to ensure that all students benefit from questioning and the resulting feedback.

# Quality Questions: Generators of Formative Feedback

*What are the features of different types of questions that produce feedback for all members of a learning community?*

Quality questions are both the initiators and the sustainers of feedback conversations, whether they lead to teacher–student or student–student interactions. Figure 5.1 features three categories of teacher questions and three types of student questions. The purpose of this framework is to guide thinking, planning, and enhanced use of questions to support learning for all. Thoughtfully prepared teacher questions are essential to the generation of formative feedback. Previous chapters make a case for the *what* and *why* of these questions, but this chapter focuses on the *how* of preparing questions to serve these different purposes.

Teacher questions alone do not guarantee student engagement in dialogic feedback. Indeed, students' questions are vital, but they are traditionally undervalued. If students are to assume the role of questioner, teachers must believe their questions important and partner with them to develop their capacity in question-asking. This chapter provides resources for teachers to use with their students as they foster student growth in this role.

## Focus Questions

These first-order questions serve as the springboard for feedback conversations. As such, they focus thinking on and establish expectations for the dialogue that follows. Most important to the formative classroom, they center teacher and student thinking on the knowledge and skills essential to advancement on a particular learning progression.

**FIGURE 5.1**

Taxonomy of Formative Questions

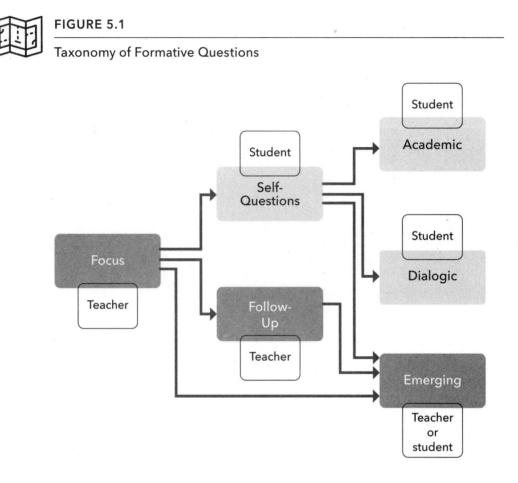

## Criteria for Quality Focus Questions

All focus questions, regardless of their specific purposes, are more effective when they meet the criteria highlighted in Figure 5.2. These criteria, sorted into four categories, can be used to create questions "from scratch" or to assess the quality of a question previously used or provided in a curriculum resource. Reflect on the four designated categories: (1) content alignment, (2) potential value of resulting feedback, (3) learner appropriateness, and (4) clarity and understandability. The first two categories relate to teacher management of curricular and instructional issues. To be useful, focus questions must be aligned with a lesson's learning target(s) and produce information that teacher and students alike can use to decide where to go next. The other two criteria address conditions that may affect students' motivation and ability to engage in thinking and responding that produce valid and reliable information.

**FIGURE 5.2**

Criteria for Questions That Stimulate Thinking and Produce Feedback for Teachers

| | Criteria | Tips for Meeting Criteria |
|---|---|---|
| **Content Alignment** | They are aligned with curriculum standard(s) and daily learning target(s). | • Connect to the essential question.<br>• Unpack learning target to identify key facts or concepts (e.g., nouns) and the level of cognitive demand.<br>• Circle back to curriculum standard to validate importance or connect the question to other components of the standard. |
| | They invite students to connect new content to prior knowledge in the subject under study or to another subject. | • Refer to previously learned content to reinforce "old" and afford connections to "new" information.<br>• Invite cross-curricular connection-making to build on student interests in other subjects. |
| | They match the level of knowledge commensurate with students' current position in the learning cycle. | • Determine whether students require additional surface learning, are prepared for deep learning, or are ready to transfer knowledge.<br>• Form questions to provide feedback at the appropriate level—surface, deep, or transfer. |
| | Cognitive demand is sufficiently high to engage students in extended thinking that leads to sustained speaking or writing. | • Ensure that questions evoke more than a two- or three-word response and are open to student elaboration.<br>• When assessing surface knowledge, for example, consider prompting students to summarize, explain, compare, differentiate, or classify instead of asking "What?" "Who?" or "When?" |
| | They incorporate academic vocabulary that connect students' informal knowledge to disciplinary knowledge. | • Identify both nouns and verbs from the standard(s) students are expected to master and incorporate them into the question/prompt.<br>• Use academic vocabulary from past lessons to reinforce students' prior learning. |

*(continued)*

**FIGURE 5.2–(continued)**

Criteria for Questions That Stimulate Thinking and Produce Feedback for Teachers

| | Criteria | Tips for Meeting Criteria |
|---|---|---|
| **Potential Value of Resulting Feedback** | They produce information needed for decisions about what to do next. | • Determine the gaps between the learning target and students' current knowledge or performance level.<br>• Develop in consideration of pivotal points in the lesson where student mastery of identified knowledge or skills is required to move forward. |
| | They generate responses that enable process-related, not task-level, feedback. | • Ensure the prompt requires students to use reasoning to construct a response.<br>• Identify the step-by-step procedures needed to reach a response to the question. |
| | They produce information that connects to next steps in learning. | • Stipulate criteria for a completely correct response.<br>• Identify possible student responses, including common misconceptions or errors, and prepare questions to reveal incorrect thinking. |
| | They produce information related to the needs of all learners (if posed to the whole class). | • Have students respond initially in writing (e.g., on a whiteboard or via an electronic app).<br>• Review individual responses to identify common errors and students who seem confused or unable to respond. |
| **Learner Appropriateness** | Questions are within students' "sweet spot" or zone of proximal development. | • Use formative feedback from previous lessons and other data as a basis for determining the level of difficulty.<br>• Plan for grappling; aim for challenge—but not frustration.<br>• Identify the teacher or peer scaffolds that might be used to close any gaps. |
| | They stimulate students to engage in reflection that surfaces related knowledge and experiences. | • Connect the content focus of the question to real life.<br>• Invite students to connect question focus to a personal experience, if appropriate.<br>• Utilize compare-and-contrast terminology to encourage connection to other concepts. |
| | They respect the social-emotional state of individual students and the class as a whole. | • Consider the social environment of your students' homes and community, and make connections as appropriate.<br>• Identify any potential "triggers" in the wording of the question that might adversely affect one or more students. |

| | Criteria | Tips for Meeting Criteria |
|---|---|---|
| **Clarity and Understandability** | They are clear, concise, and unambiguous. | • Say the question out loud to be sure it is clear and understandable.<br>• Pay attention to the syntax.<br>• Eliminate unnecessary words. |
| | They narrow and focus attention, prompting students to think about one, and only one, issue. | • Chunk big concepts into digestible bites.<br>• Construct questions that ask students to engage in one primary cognitive operation (e.g., analyze, compare, or evaluate).<br>• Refrain from running two questions together.<br>• Avoid double-barreled questions. |
| | They facilitate student connection-making. | • Precede the question with a statement that serves to focus attention and activate knowledge. Follow this with a question that invites students to make a connection to the opening statement. (Note: This helps avoid an overly complex structure for the question.)<br>• Provide students with the solution to a problem and ask what they would do to reach this answer. This alternative construction of a question encourages thinking as opposed to getting (or guessing) the "right" answer. |

**Content alignment.** Teachers formulate quality focus questions by referencing the essential content and cognitive requirements embedded in the related learning targets and curriculum standards (which are frequently multifaceted and spawn multiple learning targets). An effective learning target has a single focus area containing a knowledge and cognitive dimension, and quality questions also direct thinking to one issue. Question designers benefit by looking at the standard to which a learning target relates (to establish context and consider sequencing of questions). However, savvy designers are careful not to let standards tempt them to compromise the focus of a question by including multiple issues.

Learning targets address one of four kinds of knowledge: factual, conceptual, procedural, or metacognitive (Anderson & Krathwohl, 2001; Byrnes, 2007; Marzano & Simms, 2014). Figure 5.3 can serve as a tool for teachers considering how to unpack the knowledge dimension of a standard or target. Too often, questions prompt students to focus on facts to the exclusion of the other dimensions. This tool supports a more balanced focus within the knowledge dimension.

The most neglected dimension of knowledge is the metacognitive, which is important to the successful use of formative feedback and development of self-regulation. Consider the self-questioning, self-assessing, and self-monitoring skills identified in the previous chapter. All these skills are metacognitive. Students develop facility in using these skills through repeated use. Likewise, the corresponding dispositions tap into the metacognitive dimension. When teachers include at least one metacognitive question in a daily lesson, they help students build these important muscles for self-direction. This is essential if students are to grow in their roles as self-assessors, knowledge constructors, and collaborative contributors.

Close attention to the verbs used in a given standard is necessary but not sufficient on its own for student attainment of that learning goal. Although some standards appear to require students to simply recall a given concept or set of facts, cognitive science reminds us that if we are to remember information, then we must use or apply it. This suggests that effective formative questions require students to process information at or above level 2 of Webb's Depth of Knowledge—or the understand level of the Revised Bloom Taxonomy.

Process-level feedback activates students' thinking above the remember level, requiring them to think critically about their own thinking and learning by analyzing, comparing, connecting, or engaging in another higher-level cognitive process. As suggested, when students receive self-regulation feedback, they are similarly engaged. Given the primacy of these two levels of feedback (Hattie & Timperley, 2007), attention to cognitive demand in focus questions is critical, and that demand must be sufficient to generate student responses that help teachers form meaningful processes or facilitate self-regulating feedback.

**FIGURE 5.3**

Dimensions of Knowledge

| Dimension | Examples |
|---|---|
| **Factual knowledge** includes the building blocks of conceptual knowledge, comprising a substantial portion of surface knowledge. | • Discrete details or pieces of information (e.g., names, places, dates)<br>• Terminology |
| **Conceptual knowledge** arises out of the connections between and among facts, which include big ideas, categories, and organizers of information. | • Classifications, schema, and systems (e.g., taxonomies, literary genre, systems of government)<br>• Principles and generalizations (e.g., theorems, formulas) |
| **Procedural knowledge** focuses on how to carry out operations, which includes the steps involved in executing a task and when to apply the given procedures. | • Discipline-specific skills (e.g., using mathematical formulas, decoding while reading, kicking a soccer ball, mixing paint colors)<br>• Discipline-specific processes (e.g., reading comprehension, critical analysis in literature or art history, determination of bias in journalism) |
| **Metacognitive knowledge** relates to how thinking and learning function—more specifically, how to regulate one's own thinking and learning. | • Learning strategies (e.g., self-assessment, strategy selection, self-questioning)<br>• Self-knowledge related to one's own strengths and learning preferences |

**Potential value of resulting feedback.** *To what extent will a question engage students in thinking that leads to the surfacing of preconceptions or errors in thinking? In what ways will the question connect students to all relevant knowledge in their long-term memories?* The responses to these questions can help teachers assess the potential value of student responses as feedback. Valuable responses are informative; they reveal both the extent of students' knowledge and the depth of their thinking.

Trying out a question is the only way to determine its capacity to yield useful responses. The usual method for testing a question is to ask it in class and determine if it works. Have you ever asked a question and thought, "Wow! That was a great question. It really worked as I had imagined"? By contrast, perhaps you have had what you believed to be a well-thought-out question bomb. Most teachers have experienced both situations, but how many have documented and archived this feedback about the value of those questions? We can and we should. A file of questions that work is a treasure trove for the future.

Another strategy for testing the ability of a question to produce helpful results is collaborative brainstorming. With a group of colleagues, generate what you believe to be likely student responses to a given question. Consider how much you might learn from the responses. What if a given question yields only limited responses beyond the "correct" answer? How much will the question tell you about student thinking?

**Learner appropriateness.** Determining the appropriateness of a question begins with an understanding of students' zone of proximal development—or the "sweet spot" of learning—where the challenge is not so hard as to frustrate but not so easy as to bore. This is insightful when we reflect on the dominance of remember-level questions in many classrooms. The ZPD would not appear to have much relevance to these relatively low-level questions. The only way to help learners in this case is to default to telling them the answer or completing the task for them. Such task-level feedback has minimal long-term impact.

Designers of high-quality formative questions bring information about the current status of student learning to the task. This enables them to create questions strategically formulated to confirm suspected gaps and identify others. They also integrate information about their students' social-emotional state of being, which can be used to create questions that are more accessible and inviting.

When reviewing questions created by others, it is particularly important to ask questions such as, "Will my students be able to connect to the context of the question, or will they require background information before responding?" Sometimes it is as simple as defining a term or providing a picture to help students decipher an otherwise mysterious query. Removing barriers to student access addresses an important emotional side of student engagement.

**Clarity and understandability.** The final criterion related to a question's ability to generate useful feedback is simple, but it is often overlooked. After grappling with the more complex criteria, a question's understandability and clarity can often be determined by simply reading the question aloud and asking, "Does this make sense? Will my students understand what is being asked?" One suggested strategy for bringing clarity to a quality question is to begin the question sequence with a statement that focuses student attention on the topic and serves to activate the retrieval process.

Questions that define the course of a formative conversation are prepared in advance of class and written down in a planning document. Application of the four criteria to these questions can be accomplished in a systematic and analytical manner, and they can be applied to different question types that serve a range of purposes.

## Classroom Artifact

### Questions to Generate Student-Led Dialogue in a High School Chemistry Class

Jessica Sutherland, chemistry teacher at Vestavia Hills High School, is committed to student-driven inquiry. She makes connections between quality questioning for formative feedback and two other processes she incorporates into her chemistry classroom: POGIL (process-oriented guided inquiry learning) and ADI (argument-driven inquiry). All three feature the use of questions and collaborative group structures to support student-led investigations and dialogue. Mrs. Sutherland argues that teachers do not have to create all their quality questions from scratch; rather, they can select questions—that meet the criteria for quality and serve the intended instructional purposes—from curricula they are using.

In this lesson, students investigate equilibrium through a discussion prompted by carefully selected quality questions provided by their teacher. Mrs. Sutherland, in her role as facilitator, listens in on small-group dialogue and uses student responses as feedback regarding student progress. She asks questions if students seem stumped, but she does not provide them with answers. Students use her feedback to reflect on the process they used to create their products. They also ask one another questions and seek and use feedback from one another as they move toward the learning target.

## Types of Focus Questions

Given the primary functions of focus questions, students benefit from multiple types—namely those that activate prior knowledge and conceptions and those that reveal student thinking during different stages of learning new knowledge and skills (i.e., surface, deep, and transfer levels).

**Questions to activate prior knowledge.** Hattie and Clarke (2019) link the surfacing and assessment of prior skills and knowledge to increased learning during a lesson. They also note that the most important factor at the beginning of a lesson is teacher openness to student feedback about what they know or do not know. In addition, they lament the underuse of this question type, which can serve at least two functions: (1) making visible preconceptions students may hold about the concepts under study, and (2) stimulating student retrieval of related background knowledge they can use during new learning.

The first of the core learning principles advanced by Bransford, Brown, and Cocking (2000) is the requirement that "teachers draw out and work with the preexisting understandings that their students bring with them" (p. 19). Because "previous knowledge can help or hinder the understanding of new information," it is important that teachers help students "make their thinking visible so that misconceptions can be corrected [and they can identify] the relevant knowledge and strengths that students bring to a learning situation" (p.78). Failure to surface and address misconceptions leads to layering information on top of these. This frequently leaves students with information that may "stick" long enough for a quiz but dissipates with time as they default to their original misconceptions.

Indeed, Sawyer (2006) argues that "if teaching does not engage their prior knowledge, students often learn information just well enough to pass the test and then revert back to their preconceptions outside of the classroom" (p. 2). He also notes that "entrenched but false prior beliefs interfere with learning and need to be overcome, especially in mathematics and the physical and biological sciences" (p. 270). This is one of the primary principles underpinning the peer instruction model developed by Eric Mazur, physics professor at Harvard University, whose innovative strategies have replaced the traditional lecture-driven college classroom. He employs questions and questioning along with team-based dialogue to support students as they grapple with the misconceptions they bring to the physics classroom. Mazur's strategies are presented in print and video on Instructional Moves, a website of the Harvard Graduate School of Education (https://instructionalmoves.gse.harvard.edu/

eric-mazur). These strategies are particularly relevant to secondary science teachers, but they are informative to teachers at all levels.

All teachers can draw on past experiences to identify common misconceptions in the subject areas they teach. This is one of the benefits of collaboratively planning questions. We can also look to outside sources for guidance. For example, you can use the National Science Digital Library's science literacy maps (www.nibib.nih.gov) to review students' prior ideas about a host of science and math topics (Furtak, Glasser, & Wolfe, 2016). This rich and robust platform provides links to standards and resources for a comprehensive set of concepts. Professional associations, including the National Council for the Social Studies, the National Council of Teachers of Mathematics, and the National Council of Teachers of English, also provide helpful resources on misconceptions in their respective disciplines.

## Classroom Artifact

### Activation of Prior Knowledge in a 4th Grade Math Class

As he begins a math lesson for his 4th graders, Steven Lavender engages his students in a quick write to activate their prior knowledge. This enables him to assess their current understanding of the concepts embedded in the day's lesson. In this video, Mr. Lavender reflects on why he decided to use a quick write to open this lesson, the information derived, and how he used this feedback to inform his early moves in the lesson. By providing all students with an opportunity to make their current thinking visible through writing, he enables them to participate more effectively in the class discussion and learning activities that follow.

Beyond identifying misconceptions, these beginning-of-class questions activate individual student thinking and create a fund of knowledge on which the entire community of learners can draw. Cognitive scientists recommend that teachers tap into and build on what learners bring with them from outside the classroom as they teach new skills and concepts. The teaching of early mathematics is a case in point. Most young children have authentic experience adding and subtracting items as they engage in everyday play, but they lack the symbolic knowledge (plus and minus signs) that are taught in school. When teachers help students link their experiential early learning to formal school learning, they "acquire a more coherent and thorough understanding of these processes than if they [were taught] as isolated abstractions" (Bransford et al., 2000, p. 69).

This holds true for learning in every content area and grade level.

## *Classroom Artifact*
### The Value of Preassessment in 3rd Grade Science

Tracy Ray, 3rd grade STEM teacher at DeArmanville Elementary School, began planning a unit on fossils to modern organisms by creating the essential question *How do we know an organism is living?* Framed by reference to curriculum standards, the essential question served as a touchstone for subsequent lesson design. She committed to an intentional use of questions to obtain feedback from students throughout the unit. Mrs. Ray activated prior knowledge through two types of preassessment: determining students' knowledge of vocabulary and other key facts embedded in the standards and surfacing preconceptions.

To assess students' knowledge, Mrs. Ray created a 13-item survey. This preassessment revealed, for example, that most students understood the term *organism* but were unfamiliar with *stages of a life cycle* and *model*. She used the results for daily lesson planning and pacing.

Mrs. Ray realized that preconceptions were more important to student mastery of unit standards than knowledge of terms and facts. Therefore, to uncover these, she asked students to respond to the essential question (via an app). She viewed individual responses in real time on her device and moved around the class, posing questions to get behind erroneous beliefs such as "something is alive if it moves" and "something is alive if it is growing."

From insights gleaned through one-on-one dialogues with students, Mrs. Ray began framing focus questions for upcoming lessons:

• Is an organism still living if it is not growing?
• Can you give an example of something that is alive but not moving?
• What effect does water have on seeds?

Mrs. Ray reflected on the time and effort she invested in planning and implementing these preassessments: "In my earlier years of teaching, I might have thought that spending one entire science lesson on preassessments was a waste of our precious and limited instructional time. After taking the time to add this to my unit plan and seeing the results, I now know that a preassessment at the beginning of a new unit is extremely valuable because it allows me to... know what to do next within a unit of instruction.

"The preassessment also built student interest. [Students] began asking questions about these new terms and content areas. I was able to capitalize on the students' natural curiosity and interest by encouraging them to ask and record their questions and brainstorm ways we could discover the answers to these questions. This student investment paid dividends in the form of motivation and engagement in upcoming learning."

**Questions to generate feedback related to surface learning.** Early in a unit, students focus on the acquisition of knowledge and skills associated with mastery of a particular standard and related learning targets. Hattie and Donoghue (2016) use the term *reproductive performance* in lieu of *surface learning*, writing that "surface learning includes subject matter vocabulary, the content of the lesson, and knowing much more" (p. 3). In addition, surface learning does not equate with superficial learning or the mere memorization of facts. Rather, it is the means to the end of deeper understanding, of a learner's ability to relate one idea to another, and to see the connections within and across a subject area.

Surface learning begins with explicit instruction, often involving drill and practice. As students engage in initial learning, the appropriate feedback is at the task level and relates to a singular skill or concept required to meet a given learning target. This feedback, typically directive, focuses on a specific learning task such as decoding words, solving a simple equation, or memorizing a formula or other key facts.

Framing focus questions to gauge the extent of surface learning begins after this initial explicit instruction. If questions are to provide meaningful feedback related to surface knowledge, they are best framed above the remember level. Focus questions do not seek "just the facts"; rather, they attempt to discern the extent to which students make meaning of new facts or skills and connect these to their existing schema. To develop long-term memory of important surface knowledge, students must interpret and assimilate new information into their existing memory structures (Palincsar & Ladewski, 2006). Figure 5.4 is a tool to help you craft questions to obtain useful feedback related to surface knowledge.

**FIGURE 5.4**

Features of Questions That Generate Feedback
Related to Surface Knowledge

| Characteristics of Questions | Suggestions for Formulating |
|---|---|
| Questions focus on the core knowledge associated with the topic under study. | Unwrap the learning standard(s) to which daily learning targets relate to identify key concepts and skills. Ensure that each is addressed early in the unit by a focus question related to surface learning. |
| Questions connect to prior learning related to the concepts under study. | Embed prior learning in the question as appropriate (e.g., *Call to mind what we learned about ____ in a previous unit. In what ways might [new fact] relate to this previous learning?*). |
| Questions direct attention to the building blocks or big ideas or concepts embedded in the unit standard, essential question, and/or long-term learning targets. | Engage in backward design of questions by beginning with long-term learning targets. Generate the content focus to ensure daily lessons build toward unit outcomes. (Note: Teachers can refine and tweak focus questions as a part of their daily lesson planning. The idea here is to create an outline of questions that ensures concepts are built over time and all big ideas are addressed.) |
| Questions engage learners at DOK2 or Understand/Apply cognitive levels (e.g., clarify, paraphrase, summarize, illustrate) to assist with meaning-making. | Provide answers or solutions and ask students to create a problem (or question) that would lead to the answer. (Note: This works particularly well in math.) |

Elaborated student responses to questions that gauge surface knowledge help you decide if students are ready to move forward to more complex use of new knowledge. If students' initial responses reveal an absence of basic facts, pose lower-level questions "off the cuff" and return to direct instruction if needed. If, however, students demonstrate a basic understanding of related facts, concepts, and procedures, then they are ready to engage in deep learning.

**Questions to generate feedback related to deep knowledge.** Students engage in the construction of deep knowledge when they connect disparate concepts to one another, speculate about possible relationships between and among different phenomena, construct cause-and-effect statements, and otherwise work at a conceptual level. Carver (2006) defines *deep understanding* as "the kind of knowledge experts use to accomplish meaningful tasks," noting that such understanding "goes well beyond basic recall of facts and procedures" and involves the organization of concepts and strategies in a manner that can be used in problem solving and decision making (p. 205).

Deep learning can be initiated by inviting students to connect new knowledge or ideas to prior learning or experiences. Teachers might also ask students to compare or contrast a newly learned concept to a previously learned one. Doing so helps students make connections and concurrently provides teachers with feedback about whether students have the capacity to expand their schema. Figure 5.5 details the characteristics of questions associated with this level of processing and offers suggestions for forming such questions.

Engaging students in carefully structured inquiry is a powerful pathway to deepening their learning. This is a major premise behind project- and problem-based learning. It is also at the heart of the scientific method. The classroom artifact that follows takes us back to Tracy Ray's 3rd grade science class where her students continue their inquiry into the essential question *How do we know an organism is living?* In this segment, Tracy recounts what she learned from student claims made in response to a focus question that emerged from her analysis of preassessment data.

Questions that assess metacognitive processing are also subsumed in deep learning. These questions engage students as they reflect on their own thinking about a concept and encourage them to examine their personal schema and assess the extent to which they are deepening or expanding personal understanding. They also involve students in monitoring and self-regulating their learning. Mrs. Ray scaffolded self-regulation as her 3rd graders progressed through the unit by using proficiency scales. Her students used these learning scales throughout the unit progression and called them their "steps to success" during the self-regulation process.

**Questions to generate feedback related to the transfer of knowledge.** Transfer learning occurs when deep learning intersects with novel situations.

Questions to assess transfer go beyond the Apply level and into the Create sphere (of Bloom's taxonomy) and to level 4 of Webb's Depth of Knowledge.

**FIGURE 5.5**

Features of Questions That Generate Feedback
Related to Deep Knowledge

| Characteristics of Questions | Suggestions for Formulating |
|---|---|
| Questions prompt students to make personal meaning. | Invite students to reflect and connect to prior knowledge and out-of-school experience (e.g., *How does this expand on what you already know about ___? What criteria might be used to evaluate ___?*). |
| Questions facilitate connection-making between discrete facts or concepts (cross-disciplinary, when possible). | Ask students to speculate about cause-and-effect or evaluate/rank competing theories (e.g., *What is the relationship between ___ and ___?*). |
| Questions require students to justify, defend, extend, or elaborate on an idea. | Require textual evidence, validation of sources, or ask for an explanation of reasoning (e.g., *What evidence can you offer? Make a case for ___*). |
| Questions invite learners to assign value or make a judgment about something. | Ask students to rank/order events or natural phenomena in terms of their relative importance, requiring justification (e.g., *What criteria are you using to assess ___? What contributes to the success (or importance) of ___?*). |
| Questions provide opportunity for students to engage metacognitively. | Prompt reflective thinking that asks students to self-question or determine their preferred way of thinking about or solving a problem (e.g., *What questions do you have about ___? How would you have approached this issue had you been ___? Can you think of an alternative strategy to use?*). |

Unfortunately, the pacing of the curriculum often interferes with the provision of structured opportunities for students to engage in this type of thinking. Project- and problem-based learning seek to address this issue, and the success of these structures depends on the quality of the driving questions that guide student investigations.

## Classroom Artifact

### Reflecting on 3rd Graders' Deep Learning and Engaging Them in Metacognitive Thinking

We continued our learning about living organisms by focusing on the question *What effect does/will water have on seeds?* The students were allowed to think and write their individual claims in their science notebooks. As I walked around making observations, I noticed that 100 percent of the students claimed that because no soil was provided, the seeds would not grow in their "mini sprouters"—even if water were added. This was important feedback to me, which I used to structure the inquiry that led them to deeper learning.

While I knew that I could simply show the students an example of a seed sprouting in water only (hydroponics) or even an air plant growing without water or soil, I wanted to use this opportunity to move the students from a right-answer to a deep-learning experience through inquiry and dialogue. So, when the students were sharing their claims that the seeds would not grow or sprout, I was very careful not to interject my own knowledge into their thinking.

I have reflected that in the past I was often the biggest barrier to deeper thinking in my classroom. When I praised a student's response for being correct or incorrect, this often shut down the thinking process for the rest of the class, as well as for the speaking student. I have found that the process of guiding students' thinking to a deeper level through feedback and questioning is what allows them to make the connections to their thoughts and fuel their learning.

We discussed our "steps to success," and students took a few minutes to self-regulate and think about where they might currently fall on the learning scale and what knowledge they would have to gain to be able to move forward in their learning. There was a copy of our scale posted in the classroom, and students had individual scales in their science notebooks to which they could refer during our lessons.

Student capacity to transfer knowledge to previously unknown or novel settings is strengthened by the opportunity to engage in dialogue prompted by transfer-level questions. Such dialogue enables teachers to both scaffold instruction and obtain feedback about students' capacity to think at this level. Figure 5.6 summarizes the key features of transfer-level questions and provides suggestions for framing questions at this level.

**FIGURE 5.6**

Features of Questions That Generate Feedback
Related to Transfer Knowledge

| Characteristics of Questions | Suggestions for Formulating |
| --- | --- |
| Questions challenge students to apply learning to a new context or setting. | Create a hypothetical scenario and ask students to discuss; challenge students to create a design or develop a plan to address a real-world problem or issue (e.g., *What real-world problems or challenges might you be able to address using ____? How might you proceed?*). |
| Move students beyond the "known" and challenge them to think creatively. | Ask students to imagine a new situation to which a principle might apply or a different context in which they could use a given theory (e.g., *What if ____? Imagine that ____. What situation can you create that ____*). |

## *Classroom Artifact*

## Collaborative Planning of Quality Questions

The 8th grade ELA team at Florence Middle School discusses the value of collaboratively planning and reflecting on questions designed to generate formative feedback. They consider these quality questions to be a form of "common formative assessment." Their range of background experience enables them to identify a large bank of possible misconceptions from which they can frame questions that provide valuable feedback. Team members build on one another's strengths as they plan daily.

One team member remarks that she was not taught to prepare questions during her teacher prep program; consequently, she had been developing on-the-fly questions. She now sees the framing of quality questions to generate feedback as an important planning task. Other team members agree and note the importance of anticipating students' responses so they can be prepared with follow-up questions. These teachers point to the importance of understanding the purposes of different categories of questions—and preparing questions to serve the intended outcome.

## Follow-up Questions

A focus question is posed. Students respond—or they don't. What's next? Quality questioning that leads to formative feedback anticipates what happens next. Anticipation is an important process in effective lesson design and involves two key activities: specifying criteria for an acceptable response and predicting what students might actually say.

This process culminates in the framing of follow-up questions, which serve important functions. Namely, they make student thinking visible by inviting students to explain their reasoning; they scaffold student thinking to more correct, complete, or deeper responses; and they sustain dialogue and provide teachers and students alike with additional feedback.

The first step in framing effective follow-up questions is to stipulate the expectations for a correct/complete response to the initial question. This involves detailing the knowledge requirements and defining the expected level of cognitive processing. It is important to consider all four dimensions of knowledge: factual, conceptual, procedural, and metacognitive (Anderson & Krathwohl, 2001). Prompts that result in more complete and correct responding can address each dimension of knowledge.

Sometimes we overlook the value of advance thinking about key indicators associated with the intended level of cognitive processing. As a result, we accept student responses that include correct knowledge but inadequate processing. When we clarify precisely what the cognitive demand involves or should "sound like," we are positioned to form follow-up questions to scaffold student thinking to the intended cognitive level.

Thinking through the specifications for an expected response offers a final opportunity to assess the quality of the initial question. If teachers cannot clearly detail the knowledge and cognitive requirements, then the question requires additional work.

Having clear expectations prepares teachers to create questions that build or scaffold student knowledge and skills. Identifying the facts, concepts, and procedures required for a complete and correct response helps teachers pose follow-up questions that support students in either correcting errors or addressing omissions. Laying out the reasoning process associated with the cognitive demand supports teachers in forming follow-up questions to guide students through this process.

## Classroom Artifact

### Anticipatory Questions Scaffold
### Deep Learning for 3rd Graders

As her 3rd graders moved forward with their investigations of living organisms, Tracy Ray preplanned follow-up questions related to the focus question (*What effect does water have on seeds?*). She later reflected on the impact this follow-up questioning had on student learning:

> While the students were making their observations and discussing new developments, I began walking around the classroom asking them preplanned questions, which I hoped would give me some further feedback into their new thinking and learning and guide them to deeper thinking through dialogue with their peers. Among these questions were, "What makes you now say that your seed is growing? When you say the seed properties changed, what do you mean? What evidence can you offer to support your claim?" As I observed and listened, my students began to pull evidence from their notes on life cycles and from informational texts. They were using the vocabulary learned through the content to help them reflect and move from just a right answer to deeper thinking and learning.

Figure 5.7 is a template for use in planning follow-up questions. The classroom artifact that follows includes Tracy Ray's completed template for the example unit featured in this chapter.

**FIGURE 5.7**

Template for Preparing Follow-up Questions

| Initial (Focus) Question: | | |
|---|---|---|
| **Elements of a Correct and Complete Response** | | |
| Knowledge Requirements: | Cognitive Demand/ Reasoning Requirements: | |
| **Follow-up Questions to Take Learning Deeper** (for use after a complete and correct student response): | | |
| **Possible Responses and Related Follow-up Questions** | | |
| Possible Misconceptions | Errors in Thinking | Possible Omissions |
| | | |
| Follow-up Questions | Follow-up Questions | Follow-up Questions |
| | | |

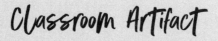
# Classroom Artifact
## Tracy Ray's Design for Follow-up Questions

*Initial (Focus) Question*: What effect does water have on seeds?

### Elements of a Correct and Complete Response

| Knowledge Requirements: | Cognitive Demand/ Reasoning Requirements: |
|---|---|
| • Organisms can be classified as living things based on the following: their ability to obtain and use resources, grow, reproduce, and maintain stable internal conditions while living in a constantly changing external environment. <br> • The life cycles of different organisms can look different, but they all follow a pattern. | • Obtain information from a variety of resources to describe organisms that are classified as living things, rather than nonliving things. <br> • Combine information to describe how organisms are classified as living things, rather than nonliving things. |

### Follow-up Questions to Take Learning Deeper
### (for use after a complete and correct student response):

• Without water, would there be the same effect on your seed? What makes you say that?

• What questions do you have about plant growth, life cycles, or seeds?

• What if a seed did not get water during its growth stage? How would that affect the stages in a seed's life cycle?

• How are the life cycles of plants connected to the water cycles?

### Possible Responses and Related Follow-up Questions

| Possible Misconceptions | Errors in Thinking | Possible Omissions |
|---|---|---|
| Seeds must have soil to begin the growth process. | Seeds are not living organisms until water is added to their seed coats. | Students can meet the learning target with a correct response but do not provide evidence or do not explain how water affects the life cycle of a plant and growth process. |

| Follow-up Questions | Follow-up Questions | Follow-up Questions |
|---|---|---|
| What causes the seed coat to soften and begin the growth process, the soil or water? What makes you say your seed is growing? | When you are sleeping, you are still living—just in a dormant state. If a seed is the embryo of a new plant and just in a dormant state, is it still living? What makes you say that? What evidence can you offer to support your claim? | What evidence can you offer to explain how water affects the life cycle of the seed in the growth process? Can you defend your statements with evidence from your learning, observations, and notes in your science notebook? When you say the seed properties changed, what do you mean? |

## Student Questions

Student questions are the richest—but least exploited—source of feedback. When students pose questions, they are communicating what they need to know or be able to do to advance their learning. Put simply, they are seeking feedback. By asking a question, students signal their willingness to engage in formative dialogue and be involved in an exchange of feedback with their teacher and classmates.

Educators have long lamented the dearth of student questions in the classroom. Rowe's (1986) "discovery" of wait time was prompted by her desire to know why students ask so few questions in science classrooms. Many factors contribute to students' unwillingness to question. Perhaps the most important is that most students don't believe this to be their job. If we want to cultivate students as questioners, we need to help them change the way they think about themselves as learners and address what Marzano (2017) refers to as their "mental states and process" (p. 5). I have investigated student question-asking and found that developing "student mindframes" is key to the development of confidence and competence in this area (Walsh, 2021). Mindframes depend on teachers being explicit with students about why they should ask questions, what types of questions support their learning, and how to frame effective questions.

## Emerging Questions

Emerging questions are those that arise spontaneously during a lesson, growing organically out of student responses. They may be posed by either the teacher or a student. When students learn to use think time 2 for reflecting on one another's responses, a larger percentage of emerging questions can be expected to come from students. Sometimes these questions eliminate the need for teacher questions since they can create a more conversational and authentic rhythm to class dialogue. Student-initiated emerging questions flourish in classrooms where students are developing the skill and the will to assume the role of questioner. In a formative classroom, teachers intentionally develop their students' capacity as questioners.

## Self-Questions

Students employ self-questions to self-regulate, which is the end goal of formative feedback. Because self-regulation is foreign to most students, it is important to teach them this process. Self-questions are also central to meta-cognition, which is the key to self-regulation. Bransford, Brown, and Cocking (2000) define *metacognition* as the process that helps "students learn to take control of their own learning by defining learning goals and monitoring their progress toward achieving them" (p. 18). These cognitive scientists credit the metacognitive approach with increases in both achievement and the develop-ment of independent learners. Hattie (2008) affirms the relationship between metacognition and student achievement ($d = 0.69$) and between self-questions and student achievement ($d = 0.64$).

## Academic Questions

As learners self-assess their progress, they sometimes identify areas of confusion and misunderstanding. At other times, they wonder how new learn-ing connects to prior knowledge. Their self-questions lead them to questions that require others' feedback, which, when posed publicly to clarify or deepen learning, are called academic questions (Walsh, 2021). Academic questions are spontaneous expressions from students of where they are in their learning, and they can serve as the most valuable form of student-to-teacher feedback. Unfortunately, they are relatively uncommon in most classrooms.

Why don't students ask more academic questions? Is it because they are not engaged metacognitively and therefore not self-monitoring to identify points of confusion or interest? Is it because of a fear or embarrassment of asking questions aloud, either because they don't believe their questions are welcome or because they lack the confidence to ask? Is it because they are afraid to reveal their "not knowing" to the teacher? Is it because students don't want to appear too interested in academics in front of their peers? Reasons differ from student to student, but all these "reasons" limit the number of questions posed by students. The result is the loss of a powerful source of feedback for all members of the classroom community.

To reverse this situation, teachers need to be intentional in developing both students' skill and will to ask academic questions aloud in class. Critical to teaching the skill of questioning is providing students with tools they can use (see Figure 5.8)—and opportunities to use those tools.

**FIGURE 5.8**

Prompts and Stems to Support Academic Questions

| Responsibility | Use When | Prompts and Stems |
|---|---|---|
| Clarify something that doesn't make sense to me. | • I don't know the meaning of a word or phrase.<br>• I am confused by wording or sentence structure.<br>• What I read or heard differs from what I thought I knew. | • How am I defining ____?<br>• What did the author mean when he/she wrote ____?<br>• What do you mean when you say ____?<br>• I thought ____. Is this incorrect?<br>• How would you summarize ____? |
| Seek to better understand the meaning of a topic or text. | • I would like an example.<br>• I would like to hear another way of explaining this. | • Can you give me an example of ____?<br>• Can you say this another way? |
| Find out more about a topic. | I would like to know more about a subject or topic. | • Where might I learn more about this?<br>• Would you elaborate on this?<br>• Please say more about this. |
| Find out if I have a complete understanding of something. | I would like to know if I have a complete understanding of an idea. | • What else do I need to know?<br>• What have I left out? |

*(continued)*

**FIGURE 5.8–(*continued*)**

Prompts and Stems to Support Academic Questions

| Responsibility | Use When | Prompts and Stems |
|---|---|---|
| Understand the relationship between two different things. | • I wonder how one thing is like (or different from) another.<br>• I wonder whether one thing might have caused another. | • How is ____ similar to ____?<br>• How is ____ different from ____?<br>• What do ____ and ____ have in common?<br>• What may have contributed to this?<br>• What resulted from this?<br>• What effect would this have?<br>• What might have caused this? |
| Determine the importance or value of something. | • I am trying to decide why something is important.<br>• I am attempting to evaluate or assess the relative importance of a person, an event, or a thing. | • How will I be able to use this?<br>• How will this help me?<br>• What makes this important?<br>• How might we go about evaluating this?<br>• What criteria (or standards) can we use to judge this? |
| Seek to understand how something might work in the real world. | • I wonder how something might help solve a real-world problem.<br>• I am trying to decide if a principle or idea has any practical value. | • Could we use this to ____?<br>• What challenges might we face if we tried to use this to ____?<br>• How might ____ affect a decision to ____? |
| Think about what might happen if an idea, a principle, or an event occurred in a different context. | • I am wondering what might happen if I changed one variable or part of a principle, rule, or concept.<br>• I want to adapt something to work in a different setting. | • What might we need to consider if we used this to ____?<br>• What if we changed ____? Would we be able to use this to ____?<br>• What if ____ happened? How would that affect ____?<br>• What could get in the way of ____ working? |

*Source:* From *Empowering Students as Questioners* (pp. 65–67), by J.A. Walsh, 2021, Corwin. Adapted with permission.

Knowing how to form questions is necessary—but not sufficient—for asking them. Students also need the opportunity and encouragement to ask. A primary purpose of think times 1 and 2 is to afford time for students to form questions and signal their desire to ask. Without these pauses, many students are simply unable to ask. As previously emphasized, teachers need to be explicit about the use of this time to form questions.

## Dialogic Questions

The purpose of this type of question is to clarify someone else's thinking or find out the rationale behind a claim or conclusion. The simplest and most effective such question is *What makes you say that?* Identified by researchers at Harvard University's Project Zero (Ritchhart, Church, & Morrison, 2011), this open-ended query invites speakers to provide reasoning, evidence, or other factors that influence their thinking. This wording is a more effective (and less threatening) probe than *Why?* or *What's your evidence?* (or other frequently used prompts). In addition, students who used this question with one another were more likely to deepen their understanding of others' perspectives and less likely to engage in argumentative talk.

Dialogic questions enable students to seek feedback that goes beyond the "correctness" of a response. Understanding the *why* behind a particular way of thinking about academic content helps learners sort and organize new information into their schema. It also supports retention and sparks deeper learning. Comprehending and appreciating why someone holds a different attitude, perspective, or point of view contributes to respect for diversity and facilitates civil discourse and disagreement. The feedback spawned by dialogic questions is the highest level of feedback, but nurturing these types of questions in the classroom is challenging.

The barriers to these questions are even greater than those for other student questions. Perhaps the greatest of these is limited exposure to dialogic questions within or outside the classroom. A right-answer orientation dominates not only classroom learning but also social and cultural issues in the broader environment. As a result, we must commit to teaching students the *why*, *what*, and *how* of dialogic questioning. The teacher's role and responsibilities in fostering dialogic questions is critical. It begins with modeling and extends to daily attention to culture-building that welcomes different ways of knowing and thinking.

Figure 5.9 includes a tool to support students as they learn to form and ask dialogic questions. (Students are more likely to ask these types of questions when we give them personal copies of this tool and routinely encourage a thoughtful review of it prior to class dialogue.)

**FIGURE 5.9**

Prompts and Stems to Support Dialogic Questions

| Responsibility | Use When | Prompts and Stems |
|---|---|---|
| Clarify the thinking of a speaker. | • I wonder how someone arrived at a certain answer or conclusion.<br>• I want to know what evidence or data a speaker is using to support his/her idea.<br>• I wonder about the steps or logic used by a speaker. | • I hadn't thought of it that way. What led you to this conclusion?<br>• Would this always be true? Can you think of something that might change your way of thinking?<br>• What makes you say that?<br>• What evidence supports this way of thinking? |
| Identify a speaker's assumptions (or beliefs). | • I wonder if a speaker's personal biases are causing him/her to overlook factual evidence.<br>• I am curious as to why someone holds a particular point of view. | • What makes you say that?<br>• What experiences have you had related to ____?<br>• I'd like to clarify your thinking about ____. |
| Surface and examine one's own assumptions. | • I am preparing to explain or defend my perspective or conclusion.<br>• I encounter a different way of thinking—one that at first seems counter to my beliefs. | • How are my personal beliefs affecting my openness to others?<br>• What has contributed to my position on this issue?<br>• Am I open to listening to this argument even though it is counter to my beliefs? |
| Challenge groupthink. | • Members of a group seem to be blindly accepting all statements and comments.<br>• I sense that members of a group are not comfortable challenging others' ideas. | • What's another way of thinking about ____?<br>• I wonder if we can think "outside the box" about this.<br>• What if we came at this issue from another direction?<br>• Imagine ____. How might this affect our thinking? |

*Source:* From *Empowering Students as Questioners* (p. 103), by J.A. Walsh, 2021, Corwin. Adapted with permission.

## Feedforward

Questions *can* serve as the catalysts for student thinking that *can* result in responses that *can* provide teachers with insight into where students are in their learning, which, in turn, leads to student engagement in the process. The three actions are conditional because each depends on the skill and will of the key players: teachers and students.

Another component of lesson design significantly affects student engagement: strategic selection of response structures. The next chapter examines the questions *How will students communicate their responses? How can I plan to secure feedback at different stages of learning? How can I strategically select response structures that support meaningful participation of every student?*

## Transferring Principles to Practice

Use Figure 5.10 to decide how you would like to use the ideas presented in this chapter to improve the quality of the questions in your classroom. Identify practices you are currently using and would like to strengthen as well as others you may wish to consider.

**FIGURE 5.10**

Transferring Principles to Practice: Questions

| Opportunities for Practice | Classroom Applications | |
| --- | --- | --- |
| | **Teacher Learning** | **Teacher Facilitation of Student Learning** |
| **Reflect on the taxonomy of formative questions (Figure 5.1) to clarify the meaning and purpose of each of the six question types.** Talk with a colleague about these, thinking about the extent to which the taxonomy makes sense to you and could be useful. | Record a selected lesson. Play back the lesson to identify the questions posed and classify each using the taxonomy. Which question type was asked most frequently? Least frequently? Is there a question type you'd like to increase? What can you do to work toward this end? | Introduce your students to the different types of questions. Explain the purpose of each type. Engage students in dialogue that focuses on how each question type supports their learning. |

*(continued)*

**FIGURE 5.10**–(*continued*)

Transferring Principles to Practice: Questions

| Opportunities for Practice | Classroom Applications | |
|---|---|---|
| | **Teacher Learning** | **Teacher Facilitation of Student Learning** |
| **Review the criteria for formulating questions with members of your team to make shared meaning.** Talk about why it might be important to use these criteria to "vet" your questions. | Use the four criteria to assess questions you plan to ask in an upcoming lesson. Edit the questions, as appropriate, to conform to the criteria. Following the class, reflect on how the criteria may have enhanced the questions and students' responses. | At the end of an identified lesson, ask your students to think back on the focus questions you asked and how well they "worked" for the students. You might record the questions on the whiteboard along with the four criteria. Begin by inviting partners to talk about the effectiveness of each question. Facilitate a sharing out with the whole class. |
| **Consider the four types of focus questions presented in this chapter.** Reflect on your own question design. Are there types of focus questions you need to emphasize? What benefits might accrue for your students? What goals can you set for yourself? | Use the appropriate tool included in Figures 5.4–5.6 to frame the question type(s) on which you've decided to place greater emphasis. Ask a colleague to use the tool to provide you with critical feedback on the questions you form. Pose these questions in the appropriate lesson, taking note of how well they work. Following the class, reflect on the quality of the feedback generated by these questions. | Talk with students about the differences between surface, deep, and transfer learning. Share a question you've designed to generate their thinking at each level. Invite students to share their understanding of the value of each type of knowledge for them personally. |
| **Talk with members of your team about the value of planning follow-up questions.** | Use the template provided in Figure 5.7 to collaboratively plan follow-up questions for a selected lesson. Commit to taking these to the classroom for potential use, recording your experiences, and debriefing their value. | At the beginning of the lesson in which you plan to try out your follow-up questions, talk with your students about the purpose of this question type. Ask them to be mindful during the lesson about how these questions support their thinking. |

| Opportunities for Practice | Classroom Applications | |
| --- | --- | --- |
| | **Teacher Learning** | **Teacher Facilitation of Student Learning** |
| **Review the three types of student questions that support formative classrooms.** Talk with colleagues about the value of working with students to increase their skill and will to pose these types of questions. | Plan minilessons to introduce students to the three types of student questions. You might chunk them out, presenting only one type during a lesson in which it is appropriate. | Reproduce the three tools for students to distribute as you instruct them in the respective question type. Decide where the students should keep the tool (e.g., in their journals, affixed to their desks, on a ring for easy access) and let them know you'll be prompting them to consult the tool as appropriate in the future. |

# Response Structures: Channels for Optimizing Responses from All

How can we select response structures to obtain relevant and accurate feedback from all students?

The goal of questioning for formative feedback is to obtain relevant information from every student that will help determine the appropriate next steps in learning. Two primary determinants of success are the quality of questions and the effectiveness of response structures. Selection of a response structure is best accomplished in tandem with the preparation of the question with which it will be used and in consideration of the broader instructional design of which it is a part.

Five specific considerations support strategic selection of response structures (Figure 6.1). The first two criteria—appropriateness to leadership responsibility and alignment with question type—serve to organize the representative alternative structures presented in this chapter. Within these two categories, attention is focused on structures that support feedback at the surface and deep/transfer levels of knowledge.

The three remaining criteria are important for all response structures, regardless of whether they are for use in whole-class or small-group activities or with surface or deep/transfer questions:

- **Accountability for all.** To what extent will this structure motivate every student to express a response and enable the teacher to match responses to students? If we want to use questioning for formative feedback, this is of prime importance.

- **Accessibility and ease of use.** Some response structures require a significant amount of advance preparation on the part of the teacher and involve new and sometimes complex directions for students. At times, the results justify this extra effort. When deciding among alternative response structures, it is important to consider whether this investment of time is warranted.
- **Advancement of peer learning.** One value of whole-class learning is the opportunity for students to interact and learn with all their peers. They can learn from both correct and incorrect responses and subsequent feedback. They also learn from their peers' questions. Further, students are positioned to receive feedback from all members of their class. Small-group structures increase and enhance the opportunities for every student to speak and listen and, as a result, can promote a higher level of engagement.

**FIGURE 6.1**

Criteria for the Selection of Response Structures

1. Appropriateness to leadership responsibility
2. Alignment with question type
3. Accountability for all
4. Accessibility and ease of use
5. Advancement of peer learning

Figure 6.2 provides a framework for thinking about the strategic selection of response structures. This framework incorporates both the "locus of control" issues (i.e., Will the dialogue be led by students, or will it be teacher-guided?) and the "level of knowledge" students will be developing.

# Enhancing Feedback During Teacher-Guided Dialogue

Teachers most frequently facilitate instruction in a whole-class setting. This traditional class organization comes with numerous advantages, including the potential for teachers to simultaneously observe and monitor all students, obtain information about the status of an entire class's progress (for the purpose of overall pacing), and provide feedback in a more efficient and equitable manner. Student benefits include opportunities to immediately access the teacher when feedback is needed, hear and profit from a wider range of teacher feedback to others, and use questions and responses from all classmates to self-assess their learning.

**FIGURE 6.2**

Strategic Selection of Response Structures

| "Locus of Control" | Level of Knowledge | |
|---|---|---|
| | **Surface** | **Deep/Transfer** |
| *Teacher-Guided* <br> • All students use initial think time to form a first response. <br> • Students may record responses in writing. <br> • Students share and compare responses as directed. <br> • Teacher monitors to receive feedback and pose follow-up questions to continue dialogue. | • All students use think time 1 to form responses. <br> • When possible, all students record or signal their responses using a selected all-response tool. <br> • Teacher monitors to identify patterns of responding. <br> • Teacher names student to respond to appropriate follow-up question and facilitates dialogue. | • All students use extended think time to form initial responses that are prompted by a focus question and supported by a teacher-selected protocol or strategy. <br> • Students record and post their initial responses and review responses of their peers. <br> • Teacher facilitates discussion by posing questions to prompt processing (e.g., analysis, synthesis, evaluation) and using strategies to engage all. |
| *Student-Led* <br> • All students use initial think time to form a first response. <br> • A selected protocol provides a structure for responding. | • All students use think time 1 for thinking and forming an initial response. <br> • Students share with one another using a selected protocol. <br> • Teacher walks around, listens in to monitor, and takes notes to record feedback. | • All students use think time 1 for thinking and forming an initial response. <br> • Students exchange ideas using an identified protocol. <br> • Teacher listens interpretively, taking notes to capture feedback. |

The perennial challenges for teachers are how to motivate all students to be ready to respond and how to secure feedback from all students at critical junctures in their learning. The first step to surmounting these challenges is to move away from the default mechanism: calling on hand-raisers who volunteer to answer. Consider replacing this with a standard process that involves four steps:

1. **Provide adequate time for all students to decode and form a silent response to questions.** Recall that the recommendation for think time 1 is a minimum of three to five seconds, but some questions (and students) need additional time. Close monitoring of students after asking a question provides clues about when most have completed thinking.

2. **Afford all students the opportunity to jot down or signal their responses before naming one student to respond publicly.** This applies primarily after you have asked a focus question to determine if the class is ready to move forward. Asking students to record their responses—using either a traditional or electronic option—serves several purposes. It helps students clarify their thinking, builds accountability, allows the teacher to review and note patterns and issues, and increases students' confidence to answer publicly if called on to do so.

3. **Ask all students to display their responses (or name one student to initiate sharing of thinking).** As public responding begins, have students compare their own thinking/responses to their classmates', using other's responses as feedback to their thinking. Students should also be ready to agree or disagree with a response if called on to do so.

4. **Monitor and interpret students' responses to decide what to do next.** As students' responses are made public, determine the current proficiency level of the class and of individual students. This is the feedback required to determine whether you should advance the lesson or decide which students, if any, need additional support.

The first two steps level the playing field by affording all students, including internal processors and second language learners, time to decode the question, search and retrieve from long-term memory, and express their thinking silently. The third step—public display of initial thinking—promotes accountability, enabling the teacher to scan all responses and allowing students to compare their responses to others and self-assess. This also provides time for teachers to determine the appropriate next step and for students to revise their responses.

During a teacher-guided questioning session, the teacher determines who talks when. Traditionally, this means oral responding by a volunteer who is called on by the teacher. In an effort to move away from a limited number of volunteers who dominate the airwaves, so to speak, many teachers instead use randomized methods (e.g., crafts sticks or electronic random number generators). The purported advantage of this method is to keep all students on alert in anticipation of being called on. A downside is the possibility of embarrassing or spotlighting a student who is painfully shy or may be adversely affected from a social-emotional perspective. One way to mitigate this is by allowing students to "pass."

A more effective approach is to use response structures that require all students to display their initial thinking simultaneously via an appropriate structure. A wide range of options can be employed for this purpose. When a teacher is helping students build surface knowledge through direct instruction, simple structures that accommodate short, closed responses are appropriate. During the development of deep or transfer knowledge, more complex and flexible structures that accommodate open-ended responses are in order. Figure 6.3 presents a representative sample of widely used structures, along with an indication of the level of learning for which each is most appropriate.

After reviewing all publicly displayed responses, the teacher taps into the responses to initiate a class dialogue designed to make the thinking behind the responses more transparent. This can proceed in one of two manners:

- The teacher can ask a question that emerges from his or her analysis of the initial responses. This may be a follow-up question, preplanned based on expected responses, or an emerging question related to an identified pattern or focused on a particularly insightful, unexpected, or novel response. Following think time 1, the teacher names a student to lead off the dialogue.
- The teacher invites students to analyze the responses to form a question they have about them, find a pattern across all responses, or identify a particular response that helped them better understand. In this case, the teacher names a student to share his or her thinking and instructs other students to listen carefully and be prepared to provide feedback and share their own thinking.

Following the initial speaker's comments, the teacher seeks to extend the dialogue long enough to uncover evidence of gaps in individual and collective understanding. The goal is to hear a range of student comments representing different levels of proficiency. Two strategies that hold potential for surfacing thinking that leads to particular responses are *revoicing* and *uptake questions*.

**FIGURE 6.3**

Sample Response Structures for Use During Teacher-Guided Questioning

| Feedback on Surface Knowledge | Feedback on Deep or Transfer Knowledge | Strategy or Protocol |
|---|---|---|
| X | | Signaled responses (e.g., hand signals) |
| X | | Choral responses |
| X | | Work samples (e.g., whiteboards) |
| X | | Response chaining |
| X | | Cooperative (e.g., numbered heads together) |
| X | | Tech-supported closed response (agree/disagree, multiple choice) (e.g., clickers, plickers) |
| X | | Tech-supported short answers (e.g., Quizizz, Mentimeter, Socrative, PearDeck) |
| X | X | Think-pair-share / think-pair-square / think-write-pair compare |
| | X | Four-square share |
| | X | Face-to-face rotations (e.g., carousel, "speed dating") |
| | X | Generate-sort-name |
| | X | Synectics |
| | X | Tech-supported (e.g., Padlet, Jamboard, SeeSaw, DoJo, VoiceThread) |

Revoicing is the act of paraphrasing a student's comment and posing a question related to that statement. This can be done immediately following the response, or it can come several turns later in the talk when it sounds like this: "Earlier, Sonya said ____. How might that connect to Henry's statement?" This teacher move encourages students to make connections and take their thinking deeper. Resulting responses offer feedback related to students' ability to engage in this level of thinking.

Uptake questions incorporate some element of a student's response in a request for further elaboration (Juzwik, Borsheim-Black, Caughlan, & Heintz, 2013), thereby shifting "responsibility for thinking back to the students [so as] to encourage student elaborations and increase student thinking and engagement" (Michener & Ford-Connors, 2013, p. 91). This strategy can be used to uncover student reasoning and reveal the process used to determine a response. Use of this strategy provides information needed for the teacher to offer process feedback.

Teacher-guided questioning positions the teacher as a facilitator. The facilitation guidelines and moves can be adapted to questioning to secure feedback at all levels of learning—from surface to transfer. Appropriate response structures can be integrated into the overall lesson design where needed to increase students' engagement and feedback to the teacher and to one another.

## Structures to Secure Feedback on Surface Knowledge During Teacher-Guided Lessons

Teacher-guided questioning is the go-to mode during direct instruction when students are building foundational knowledge or developing new skills. Securing feedback at critical junctures in new learning is key to teacher and student success. Teachers can select from three categories of structures as they plan how to obtain feedback during this phase of learning.

### Signaled Responses

Students can use simple gestures to communicate the status of their thinking quickly and efficiently. A popular example is thumbs-up/thumbs-down, which is used in many classrooms as a quick check for understanding. Whether this yields reliable information, however, is in question. This practice can become so routinized that students respond with little thought and sometimes give a thumbs-up just to "stay under the radar." Many elementary teachers adopt and teach their students a more finely tuned set of signals to both wean them from hand-raising and obtain feedback from each student about where they are in their thinking. Figure 6.4 illustrates the hand signals adopted by one school. It is important to adopt schoolwide signals to ensure continuity between classrooms (including PE, art, music, and other enrichment classes) and grade levels.

**FIGURE 6.4**

Sample Gestures for Student Feedback

I'm still
thinking.

I'm ready to
respond.

I agree with
the speaker.

I respectfully
disagree.

I have a
question.

One school developed a set of feedback paddles for students to use as they provide feedback after think time 2 (Figure 6.5). Beginning in kindergarten, students were taught to listen actively to their classmates and prepare to respond with feedback to the speaker. To achieve this, teachers intentionally taught their students to use public speaking voices when responding to a question or making another whole-class contribution.

**FIGURE 6.5**

Feedback Paddles

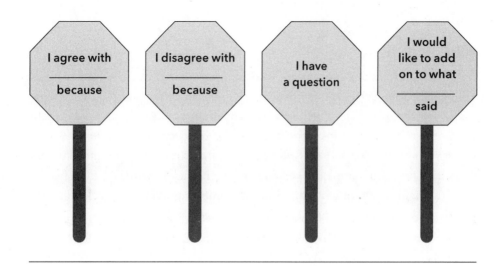

A final approach to gesturing involves students standing and responding to teacher questions using arm movements modeled by the teacher. For example, during an elementary math lesson, teachers might read a problem and ask students to show whether they should add, subtract, multiply, or divide by forming the appropriate operation symbol with their arms. During ELA, the teacher might ask students to use gestures or arm movements to show the proper punctuation mark for a sentence. This approach benefits students since standing up and moving around gets more oxygen to the brain (thereby energizing them).

Secondary teachers adopt more age-appropriate strategies. For example, substituting fist to five (where one's fist signifies "not at all" and five fingers means "to a great degree") helps students communicate how much they understand a given concept or idea. Many teachers use the four corners strategy where each corner represents a different response. Students move to the appropriate corner and talk with their classmates about why they responded as they did. Similarly, asking students to line up on a continuum (from 1–10) in response to a given question affords an opportunity for a more fine-tuned response—as well as the chance to talk with classmates about why they chose a particular rating.

Stop light is another strategy used in many classrooms. Each student is provided with a set of cards or plastic cups—red, yellow, and green—with which to signal their level of understanding at a given point in a lesson. Students place the green card/cup on their desks as long as they are comprehending lesson content. Should they need the teacher to slow down or explain further, they put the yellow card/cup on their desks. Red signifies a student's need for reteaching or direct assistance.

## Work Samples

Work samples are appropriate when a question calls for students to apply knowledge or skills. This may involve solving a mathematical problem, punctuating or diagramming a sentence, or any other work product. When teachers want students to display their responses, they employ whiteboards (or a similar electronic tool). If the intent is to walk around and monitor student work, this can be as simple as working on paper or a laminated desktop (which enables larger writing). Not only do work samples provide feedback to teachers, they can also be used for peer review and feedback.

Technology expands the possibilities and potential of work samples. Google Docs and Pear Deck, for example, offer space for simultaneous recording by students and allow the teacher to archive responses. The caveat here is not to use such devices as worksheets. Within the context of questioning for formative feedback, the idea is to engage a real-time review of students' responses to determine immediate next steps with the class and individual students.

## A Special Kind of Fishbowl in a Kindergarten Class

Sue Noah, kindergarten teacher at Athens Elementary School, frequently uses pairs to organize student learning in her classroom. During this math lesson on counting, pairs work together to share their strategies. Mrs. Noah uses this as an opportunity to listen in and observe her young students at work. When she identifies students whose thinking may be instructive to their classmates, she has the class circle around the spotlighted pair by exclaiming, "Macaroni and cheese, everybody freeze!" She then invites the entire class to join her and listen to the identified students' explanations.

## Cooperative Responses

Stopping to allow students to interact with their peers serves multiple functions within the context of direct instruction. It allows learners to reflect on and process new learning as they speak and listen to one another; it also permits students to give and receive feedback to one another. This can be beneficial, particularly if students know they will each be accountable for sharing a response if called on to do so.

Two strategies that promote this end are think-pair-share and numbered heads together. These two strategies are flexible and can be adapted for use in all content areas and at all instructional levels, K–12.

Think-pair-share (TPS) is most effective in checking for understanding of surface knowledge when it is governed by a protocol—step-by-step directions that ensure equitable responsibility for participation and a clear understanding of responsibilities. When used during direct instruction, the teacher guides students through the protocol, reinforcing expectations at each turn.

TPS is most appropriately used to secure feedback on questions requiring an elaborated response, and it is distinguished from the simpler turn-and-talk strategy that can be used spontaneously for quick processing or check-ins with peers. Many teachers assign partners to work together over the course of a week (sometimes longer) to reduce transition time and help build comfortable relationships.

# Featured Protocol: Think-Pair-Share (TPS)

*(directions for students)*

Find your TPS partner and a comfortable place to stand. You'll be speaking and listening to each other to check your understanding of an important concept related to today's learning target. I'll provide directions about when you should speak and when you should listen. I'll also be the timekeeper. When it's your turn to speak, you should use your entire time, even if you have to repeat yourself to fill your time. You can also use your time to ask a question you'd like your partner to answer when it's their time to speak.

*(directions for teacher)*

1. Designate partner 1 and partner 2 within each pair.

2. Say, "The question I'd like each of you to think about is _____. Take ten seconds or so to think about what the question is asking and decide what you think."

3. Tell partner 1, "You have one minute to tell your partner what you think in response to the question." Then tell partner 2, "Your job is to listen carefully to be able to paraphrase and provide feedback." Time varies with the complexity of the question and student age. Thirty seconds is often appropriate for younger students, whereas secondary students can profitably use up to two minutes for more complex questions.

4. When the allocated time expires, say, "Partner 2, now it's your time to speak. Begin by paraphrasing what you understood your partner say. Partner 1, give a thumbs-up if your partner got it right. Partner 2, continue talking to share your response to the initial question."

Following the TPS exchange, the teacher can either allocate additional time for discussion (during which the partners may be asked to decide what to share with the whole group and who will report) or move directly to whole-group sharing and discussion. In the latter case, teachers find it productive to ask students to share their partners' thinking. This promotes active listening and can increase the confidence of a reluctant speaker to participate.

Among the variations of TPS are think-pair-share-square, which places two pairs together to compare their thinking prior to whole-class sharing, and think-write-pair-share, which affords more time and accountability for individual thinking prior to partner sharing. Grade, maturity level, and nature of the academic content are factors that influence the most appropriate choice of strategies.

Regardless of which variation is used, TPS is most effective when it culminates in whole-class sharing. This allows expanded peer feedback and broadens the impact of teacher-to-student feedback. Additionally, TPS prepares all students for participation in whole-group dialogue through advance thinking and listening to peers. In short, TPS is a highly adaptable strategy that can be employed to assess deep knowledge.

Numbered heads together is another cooperative response that can be used to check for understanding of surface knowledge. Students work in groups of four to six, which are strategically created with attention to group chemistry. Group members talk together to reach a consensus response to a teacher question. Each group member must be prepared to respond because the teacher uses a random selection process to call on students.

Prior to this, the teacher prepares a set of questions, organizes groups, and decides whether to use a die or some other random number generator for respondent selection. The number and type of questions prepared depends on where students are in the learning cycle. The suggestion is that at least one focus question (at the understand level or above) be featured. Related remember-level questions can be used to reinforce factual knowledge and prime the pump for a lengthier dialogue about the focus question.

Numbered heads together provides an opportunity for not only peer feedback but also feedback to the teacher about where a class is in its learning. The teacher is also positioned to provide feedback to correct or reinforce learning for all students. This structure can be used effectively when students are learning new information and would benefit from both small-group, peer-to-peer feedback and whole-class feedback from the teacher. This strategy can also facilitate the correction of misunderstandings and support efficient review to determine student readiness for a summative assessment.

# Featured Protocol: Numbered Heads Together

*(directions for students)*

We will be using numbered heads together to assess where we are in our learning. You've been assigned to a small group where you'll talk together to reach a response to questions I'll pose. I expect each of you to participate in your group's dialogue and to be sure that you agree with and understand the group's response. In a minute, I'll ask you to number off in your groups, 1–4. After your group has time to come up with a response, I'll roll a die and call out a number. If that is your number, you'll raise your hand.

I'll then name someone with a raised hand to offer the first response to the question. What kinds of questions, if any, do you have about this process?

*(directions for teacher)*

1. Thoughtfully organize students into small groups of four (up to six, depending on the total number in a class and the maturity level of students). Then have group members number off, counting 1–4. Tell them to remember their number, jotting it down if they need to.

2. Ask the first question aloud, projecting it on a screen if possible.

3. Have group members talk to one another to come to an agreement on a response. Afford a reasonable amount of time for group talk, and call time.

4. Say, "Now I'm going to roll my die. Would all the [number] please raise your hands?"

5. Call on one student with a raised hand. You may choose to number the groups and randomly select the group number of the student who is to respond.

6. Say, "Everyone listen carefully as [student] answers to decide if your group agrees."

7. After the student responds, ask, "Would others who have this number raise your hands if you agree with what [student] said?" Pause, and then name a student to elaborate on the previous response if appropriate. If there are groups that do not agree, select one reporter to share that group's response and rationale.

8. Bring this round to a close by affirming the correct response and soliciting additional dialogue about the concept if desired.

9. Move to the next question, following the same protocol.

## Response Chaining

Marzano has popularized the use of the term *response chaining* for a response structure that promotes active listening and builds accountability (Marzano & Simms, 2014). Teachers inform students of their responsibility to listen to one another and decide whether they agree or disagree with a speaker. Students know they are subject to being randomly called on after a classmate has spoken to paraphrase his or her response and indicate whether they agree or disagree. If they agree, they are expected to add to or provide reasons for their agreement. If they disagree, they must indicate the reason for their disagreement and offer their own thinking. Marzano suggests that the chain can be extended through several students, depending on the complexity of the question and the lesson's purpose. This strategy is best used as students are solidifying surface knowledge and in response to an understand/apply question.

Response chaining provides a structure for scaffolding student engagement in the whole class. By retaining control of who speaks when, teachers build the norm of equitable participation, addressing the oft-mentioned concern that discussion allows a few students to monopolize. Additionally, by requiring the paraphrase, students know they are responsible for actively listening. Finally, the requirement of providing evidence, whether in agreement or disagreement with the previous speaker, moves students to more elaborated responses. This protocol requires commitment and intention from the teacher and an understanding of both the procedures and the rationale by students.

## Tech-Supported Response Systems

Technology supports quick and easy checks for understanding in whole-class settings. An increasing number of apps, platforms, and devices allow teachers to obtain both closed-choice and short-answer responses to their questions. Some of the more popular systems (at time of writing) are Plickers, Socrative, Clickers, Mentimeter, Pear Deck, and Quizizz. The choice of system you use is an individual (often a schoolwide) one and is influenced by cost, ease of use, and appropriateness to a given age group and subject area.

Most teachers recommend identifying a limited number of systems that meet the formative assessment needs for a given group of students and using them routinely to reduce the amount of time required to address logistical and management issues. It is also important to evaluate the extent to which the information produced supports instructional decision making. These response structures, like their traditional (i.e., nontech) counterparts, are a means to the end of procuring formative data from all students.

## Classroom Artifact

### Integrating Tech Responses into Whole-Class Discussion

Jesse Snider, 8th grade ELA teacher at Florence Middle School, balances opportunities for students to speak and listen during class dialogue with the use of tech tools to provide simultaneous feedback from all. He believes a carefully designed lesson can effectively incorporate both. In this lesson (designed to develop students' skills with text evidence), he incorporates the use of Pear Deck with partner talk and whole-class discussion. He notes that digital platforms offer students anonymity in responding, which can contribute to their comfort in sharing. In turn, feedback that affirms their responses contributes to their confidence, which encourages them to share aloud. Digital platforms let him know where every student is at a given point in a lesson so he can decide what next. He believes, however, that these tools are not a substitute for class dialogue, which provides an opportunity for students to make their thinking visible and take their thinking deeper.

## Structures to Secure Feedback on Deep Knowledge During Teacher-Guided Lessons

Whole-class discussion is a means by which teachers can scaffold deep learning through questioning and feedback. Incorporating strategies and structures into the design of this type of discussion can serve to engage all students in thinking and responding, which in turn supports both teacher-to-student and student-to-student feedback.

### Initial Written Responses

One method for deepening discussion is to begin by inviting all students to reflect on a focus question, form an initial response, post their thinking publicly, and then scan classmates' responses as they prepare to interact with one another. Public posting of responses enables students to compare others' thinking to their own as they prepare to build on one another's thinking during discussion.

Individual recording and publishing can be accomplished via a tech-supported or a paper-and-pencil option. Keep in mind that, when tapping into deep knowledge, the app or platform must accommodate lengthier responses. Two examples are Padlet and Jamboard. Low-tech options include writing on sticky notes or wall charts. A range of protocols can support thinking and responding. The following examples can prime the pump for whole-class discussion.

**Four-Square Share.** This structure helps students exchange perspectives with peers within a tightly controlled set of procedures. The teacher prepares or has students create a simple template for note-taking prior to beginning the activity. The graphic organizer is essentially a quadrant with a rectangle super-imposed in the center. Before the lesson, the teacher organizes students into groups of four. Students read a short passage and then jot down their ideas to a prompt in one of the four boxes. The prompt can be as simple as "Identify the most important ideas in this passage." It could also be a more complex teacher-generated focus question. The teacher allocates an appropriate amount of time for reading and recording.

One student begins by sharing his or her ideas. While the speaker shares, other group members record what they understand the student to be saying. (It is important to stress that students are not dictating to one another; rather, they are actively listening to make meaning of what their classmates are say-ing.) The teacher may serve as timekeeper, allowing 30–60 seconds for each student's initial response and indicating when talk should move clockwise to another speaker who then has an equal amount of time to talk. This continues until all four group members have shared (and their peers have listened and taken notes). The teacher then instructs students to silently and individually reflect on what they now think about the question. Students write a few sen-tences to summarize their thinking. The teacher can invite whole-class dia-logue, encouraging students to continue to edit and expand their thinking as they listen to classmates outside their quads. Many teachers ask students to turn in their note-taking templates so they can assess the extent to which stu-dent thinking deepened over the course of the lesson.

**Ink Think.** This protocol invites silent reflection and the recording of ideas on wall charts prior to the initiation of speaking and listening. It works well at the beginning of a unit to activate existing conceptions, as a midpoint check for understanding when transitioning from surface to deep learning, and toward the end of a unit to facilitate connection-making and closure.

Before class, the teacher identifies focus questions or big ideas related to the unit under study and writes each one in the center of separate wall charts (typically 4 feet × 4 feet) arranged around the room. Multiple questions or ideas related to the unit serve as prompts for thinking and recording. The teacher also assigns students to small groups of four to six members, taking care to ensure a balanced mix of students in each group. Finally, the teacher organizes and distributes different colored markers to each group. Group members should use the same marker as they rotate from chart to chart.

As students work at the wall charts, the teacher walks around, monitoring students and recording evidence of individual and group effectiveness, including (1) individual student contributions, (2) the extent to which group members build on one another's ideas, (3) each group's efforts to build on the thinking of other groups (during the rotations), and (4) the quality of each group's closing dialogue and processing of ideas. During this time, the teacher also makes a final decision about the questions to be posed during whole-class discussion, which might include one or more of the original focus questions or questions that emerge during the ink think activity.

# Featured Protocol: Ink Think

*(directions for students)*

Today, we will use ink think, a protocol designed to prompt your thinking about the big ideas in this unit. You will work silently with members of your group to respond as completely as possible to the prompt. As you record your ideas, you will create a web or concept map to illustrate the connections between the ideas you generate. Your responses will let me know the depth of your individual and collective knowledge about the big ideas in this unit.

*(directions for teacher)*

1. Have students read their group's prompt and take two minutes to jot down their thinking before moving to their assigned charts.

2. Instruct students to silently move to their designated wall chart. Their marker color should match the writing color in the center of the chart.

3. Have students silently record their ideas on the chart.

4. Say, "As you continue working, read and think about your group members' responses. If one of your ideas connects to one recorded by a classmate, connect your idea to it with a line. If you have the same idea or if you agree with someone else's idea, place a checkmark beside it." If you disagree or have a question, place a question mark beside the item.

5. Have students continue to work silently, using their classmates' contributions to spur additional thinking.

6. Call time after two or three minutes have passed. Instruct each group to move clockwise to the next chart, where they will review another group's question and responses.

7. Tell students to place a checkmark beside the ideas with which they agree and a question mark beside any for which they have questions. They should also add their own responses to this wall chart, continuing to use the webbing process.

8. Give students two minutes to review and add to this chart.

9. Repeat this process until each group has had an opportunity to respond to all questions and add their thoughts to each wall chart.

10. Say, "Return to your initial station and review the additions to your chart made by the other groups. After a minute for silent review, talk together to synthesize responses and generate questions you may have."

11. Have students return to their desks for whole-class discussion.

Ink think is a variation on a more widely known and used response structure: carousel. Like ink think, carousel involves the organization of students into strategically formed small groups of four to six students. Small groups of four are optimal for elementary classrooms; some secondary classes can function effectively in somewhat larger groups. Carousel also begins with team members forming and writing initial responses to an assigned question on wall charts.

During carousel, unlike ink think, team members speak and listen to one another, agreeing on group responses. This response structure benefits from role assignments, including group facilitator, recorder/reporter, and timekeeper. Finally, like ink think, carousel involves group rotations that permit students to learn from and add to the thinking of other groups and culminates with groups returning to their initial stations for an analysis and a summary of all responses.

Although the two response structures share many of the same features, they are not necessarily interchangeable. Decision making about which to use when relates to lesson purpose and student skill level. If the purpose is to ensure accountability in responding for all students, ink think may be the preferred structure. However, if the purpose is to engage students in speaking and listening, respectfully agreeing and disagreeing, and reaching consensus, then carousel is the structure of choice.

## Classroom Artifact
### Use of Carousel with 1st Graders to Support Dialogic Feedback

First grade teacher Kate Armstrong establishes small groups of four to rotate through stations during a math lesson on shapes. Students engage in small-group dialogue and record their insights on chart paper. Mrs. Armstrong uses the feedback she receives from students to engage them in discussion by posing follow-up questions. She uses think times as she takes the thinking of these young students deeper.

**Generate-Sort-Name.** This protocol lends itself to prompts that require students to generate multiple responses to open-ended questions. For example, it might be the response structure of choice when a question asks students to think of several possible causes of a particular outcome, attributes associated with a character, or solutions to a given problem. As in ink think, students begin with silent reflection and writing before recording each idea on a separate sticky note. Students then work silently in small groups of three or four to share their thinking. They place their sticky notes on a sheet of chart paper and collaboratively group items together to form categories. This protocol culminates with an opportunity for students to talk together about their groupings, add additional items to the groupings (if desired), and name the categories. At this point, the teacher leads the whole class in a sharing-out activity.

Throughout the process, the teacher circulates and observes or listens in to group work, taking notes on individual contributions and group interactions (and keeping students on track with directions as needed). These observations can provide important formative feedback on individual participation and collaborative skills. The teacher can also look for misconceptions or errors on the charts, placing a question mark beside the relevant comment or engaging students in conversation by asking questions such as *What makes you say that?*

During the latter phases of small-group work, the teacher makes a final decision about the question(s) that will focus the whole-class discussion. This discussion could be sparked by simply asking *In what ways did your participation in this process change your thinking about our focus question?* This question asks for student reflection on feedback to their thinking, which is one of the important benefits of this exercise.

## Featured Protocol: Generate-Sort-Name

*(directions for students)*

We will use a protocol that begins with individual silent thinking and recording of ideas on sticky notes. Each of you has some sticky notes to use while you work on your own to generate as many responses to the focus question as you can. Please write legibly because your classmates will be reading what you write. I'll lead you through this activity, which begins with your individual work, then asks you to share within a small group, and ends with a whole-class discussion.

*(directions for teacher)*

1. Say, "You have the next two or three minutes to record as many ideas as you can on your sticky notes. Remember to work independently and silently. Write only one idea per sticky note, and write legibly."

2. When most students have stopped writing, give directions for them to work in small groups: "At this point, you'll begin sharing with others in your group. You'll continue to work silently by placing your sticky notes on the chart paper. Your group's job is to place like ideas together on the chart."

3. Prompt students to move the sticky notes around to create categories of like ideas. Point out that they can move one another's sticky notes and change their minds about how to best group the items. They should not be afraid to group and regroup.

4. Say, "As you work, other ideas may occur to you. When they do, grab a sticky note, record the new idea, and place it in the group where you believe it belongs."

5. After three or four minutes—or when most groups appear to have created their initial groupings—ask students to pause for additional directions: "Most of you seem to have completed your initial sorting. Now you may talk with one another about what's on your chart and decide if your groupings make sense. Does every item in each group belong? If not, do you need to create a new group, even if there's only one item in it? Can you add anything to any of your groups? If so, have someone record the new idea on a sticky note and add it to the chart. Are any of your categories too big? Can you break them into smaller categories that would make sense?"

6. Have students come up with a one- to three-word name for each of their categories. They should draw a circle around each category and write its name above.

7. When all groups have completed their work, provide directions for a gallery walk: "We'll now begin a gallery walk. You'll move as a group to look at other groups' responses. Closely examine their charts to look for similarities and differences. Share your observations with your group. You may want to take pencil and paper so you can jot down notes to use later in our class discussion."

8. Direct groups to move in a clockwise direction to view other groups' products. Afford them one or two minutes at each of the other stations.

**Synectics.** This protocol invites students to make connections between a big idea or concept under study and seemingly dissimilar ideas through metaphorical thinking. The purpose is to encourage creative connection-making prior to a whole-group discussion.

Begin by identifying the concept you want students to think about more deeply. Prepare a question designed to activate student thinking and writing. Then generate a set of unlike concepts or processes to which you want students to compare the selected big idea. Prepare a graphic organizer to facilitate independent thinking and writing (Figure 6.6).

Instruct students to respond individually and silently to the prompt. Allocate time appropriate to the prompt and students. Then direct students to think about each of the metaphors, jotting down ways in which they believe each is like the concept in question. Ask students to select the one that best represents their understanding of the concept.

**FIGURE 6.6**

Synectics Example

Jot down as many ideas as possible in response to the following question:

*What are the primary challenges of sustaining a military alliance such as NATO?*

Think about ways in which sustaining an alliance is like each of the following. Jot down your thinking for each in the space provided.

| Beekeeping | Gardening |
|---|---|
| Protecting a Coral Reef | Coaching a Team |

Students can then work in small groups of three to five members to share their thinking and collectively select their favorite metaphor. Alternatively, you can post chart paper displaying the choices around the room and invite students to move to the paper that matches their choice. Should you choose this approach, direct students to name a recorder/reporter and create a list of ways in which the concept is like the selected metaphor. Circulate to listen in on small-group conversations, taking note of the depth of student understanding. At the end of the time allocated for small-group sharing, facilitate a whole-class discussion that draws from the work of small groups.

## Whole-Class Discussion

The protocols in the previous section are examples of structures that can potentially engage every student in giving and receiving feedback prior to a whole-class discussion. These and other structures also prime the pump for deeper dialogue with more balanced participation. When leading a discussion intended to develop and assess deep knowledge, the teacher's role shifts from an expert who provides corrective feedback to a facilitator who withholds evaluative feedback unless students allow errors of fact or reasoning to go uncorrected. Dillon (1988) warns that validating feedback can terminate thinking and speaking. When a teacher affirms a student's response, the speaker and listeners conclude that the teacher has heard the "correct" response he or she wanted. As a result, the opportunity for deeper thinking is lost.

Therefore, teachers should use alternatives to direct feedback to sustain students' thinking and speaking. Maximizing student talk (and minimizing teacher talk) serves to deepen student thinking and learning. Each of the alternatives in Figure 6.7 is an efficient and effective method for accomplishing this goal.

**FIGURE 6.7**

Nonevaluative Responses to Student Comments During Discussion

| Alternative | Comments |
|---|---|
| Use think time 2. | Use this prior to making any comment. The recommended pause during discussion is a minimum of five seconds—longer if the question or student comment is complex. |
| Paraphrase what you heard the student say (e.g., "You said…."). | This is particularly appropriate when you notice puzzled looks from other students. |
| Describe your state of mind (e.g., "I am curious about…."). | This positions the teacher as a co-inquirer and discussant. |
| Invite the speaker to elaborate (e.g., "Can you say more about…?"). | This request can serve to clarify and take student thinking deeper. |
| Invite the speaker to pose a question (e.g., "What question would you like to ask your classmates?"). | Inviting the speaker to pose a question to others is a strategy to extend his or her thinking and sustain discussion. |
| Invite listeners to pose a question to the speaker or the class (e.g., "Let's pause, reflect on what's been said, and identify unanswered questions"). | This is a productive strategy to use as a discussion ends. Students can record their questions in a shared doc or jot them down to turn in as an exit ticket. These can serve as valuable formative feedback regarding where students are in their thinking. |

# Enriching Feedback During Student-Led Dialogue

Student opportunities to assume responsibility for questioning, dialogue, and feedback within collaborative groups can enhance both self-regulation and what Bailey and Heritage (2018) call coregulation. This also contributes to individual and collective efficacy, which are associated with effective use of feedback. In addition, student-led dialogue lends itself to the development of deep knowledge and transfer.

The role of the teacher during student-led dialogue is to collect evidence (feedback) through close observation and careful listening and to monitor student interactions, intervening only when needed to ensure adherence to norms and the protocol. Student-led discussions are most appropriate for students in 5th grade and above; however, a number of protocols can be adapted for use with younger students. Their effectiveness depends on the time and effort invested in conveying expectations and norms. Participation in teacher-guided dialogue, especially those supported by protocols, prepares students for this self-guided work.

Five protocols are described in the sections that follow. They are representative of a larger body of structures that can be tapped, but these five are adaptable across content areas and grade levels.

## Reciprocal Teaching

Reciprocal teaching is a scaffolded discussion protocol that engages small groups of students in four important processes that build understanding: clarifying, questioning, summarizing, and predicting. Developed by Palincsar and Brown in 1984 to improve reading comprehension, a large body of research has substantiated its effect on student achievement. Sawyer (2006) observes, "Reciprocal teaching helps students recognize the questions they need to ask themselves as they are trying to understand something they are reading" (p. 7). This protocol builds the skills students need to assume the role of self-assessor and move toward self-regulation.

Students are organized into groups of four and assigned short readings. Over the course of four rounds, students assume each of four roles: clarifier, questioner, summarizer, and predictor. They read the assigned portion of a text through the lens of their respective roles and share their thinking. They then switch roles and continue reading. Teacher modeling and scaffolded practice are prerequisite to students' independent use of the process. For further reading, Lori Oczkus (2018) offers a comprehensive examination of this protocol in *Reciprocal Teaching at Work.*

## Reflective Questioning

Another structured small-group protocol that functions through differentiated roles is reflective questioning. This structure supports student dialogue intended to deepen thinking and understanding. It can be adapted for use in all core content areas and is most effective in 5th grade and above. The success of this protocol, like other small-group structures, depends on group composition and preteaching strategies associated with each role. This structure is best used with a question that has a high cognitive demand following student acquisition of a breadth of surface knowledge on a given topic.

As triads of students are working, the teacher can obtain rich and deep feedback about each student's current level of thinking. Evidence of each student's contributions can be recorded on a prepared template. The teacher's role is to circulate and listen, record observations, and serve as timekeeper. At the end of three rounds, the teacher can bring closure by summarizing some of the key ideas that were voiced during the activity and having students share what they learned from their peers.

### Featured Protocol: Reflective Questioning

*(directions for students)*

Today, you'll be working in groups of three to think more deeply about one of the big ideas in this unit. Everyone will begin by silently and independently jotting down thoughts related to the focus question. You'll have the chance to deepen your thinking by assuming each of the following roles during one of three rounds of talk: reflector (the primary speaker who shares an initial response to the question), questioner (the listener who asks questions to help the reflector dive deeper into their thinking), and feedback provider (the observer who listens actively to the two speakers and takes notes about how the questioner helps the reflector).

*(directions for teacher)*

1. Have students read the question and jot down their thinking. Explain that they can reference these notes when it's their turn to speak.

2. Assign roles for the first round. The three roles and related responsibilities are as follows:

• **Reflector:** You will begin by sharing your initial thinking about the question. You'll be talking to the questioner who will ask questions to clarify and take your thinking deeper. Be sure to pause occasionally to give the questioner a chance to pose questions.

• **Questioner:** Your job is to listen actively to the reflector, jotting down notes if you need to. Ask questions to clarify and take the speaker's thinking deeper. You may want to use some of the question stems you've used during class such as *What examples can you offer? What makes you say that? What led you to this conclusion?* and *What evidence supports this thinking?* Remember, your job is to ask questions—not to get involved in the discussion at this point.

• **Feedback Provider:** Your primary job is to listen actively and take notes. You are not to speak as the reflector and questioner interact with each other. You'll provide feedback later. Listen to identify questions that take the reflector's thinking deeper and ideas presented by the reflector that take your own understanding deeper.

3. Each round of talk will be three minutes. During this time, the reflector will share his or her thinking and respond to questions posed by the questioner. Call time at the end of three minutes.

4. Say, "It's now the feedback provider's turn to speak. Give feedback to the reflector focused on how their thinking helped your understanding. Share any questions posed by the questioner that you think helped the reflector go deeper. You have one minute to offer your feedback."

5. Have students change roles. Once again, provide three minutes for the reflector-questioner interaction. Call time when the feedback provider is to report.

6. During the third round, students should assume the role they haven't had yet. Repeat the process.

## Inside-Outside Circles

This widely used structure divides a class into two groups whose members are seated in concentric circles. Each group has an opportunity to discuss when seated in the inside circle and to listen closely and observe when seated in the outside circle. There are a number of protocols using this basic organization (e.g., Paideia seminars, Socratic circles, and variations of a more generic fishbowl discussion), which are compared in more details in *Questioning for*

*Classroom Discussion* (Walsh & Sattes, 2015). That book also offers strategies for teaching students the skills required for productive participation in a student-driven dialogue.

The inside-outside circle protocol has the potential to support a range of feedback interactions. Students within the inside circle give and receive feedback to one another as they engage in dialogue. Students in the outside circle can provide feedback to one or more students in the inner circle. Listening students also provide one-to-one feedback to their assigned speakers at the conclusion of the discussion. The teacher, who is in the role of observer and active listener, interprets student comments to determine the extent to which students are developing deep knowledge. Inside-outside structures afford students the opportunity to reverse roles during a second round. At the end of two full rounds, students can reflect on how they will use peer feedback to deepen their learning, bringing the feedback loop full circle.

## Table Rounds

Table rounds is a structure that enables small groups of four students to engage in open-ended dialogue centered on one focus question provided by the teacher. Within a class, several conversation groups, each addressing a different focus question, work concurrently. At the end of the allocated time for discussion (generally five to six minutes), students rotate to a different table, review the previous group's work, provide feedback, and then build on those contributions.

Two organizational features provide structure for these small-group conversations: group roles and norms. The roles and responsibilities featured in Figure 6.8 offer opportunities for student leadership in this free-flowing dialogue, and the sample norms in Figure 6.9 serve to reinforce the importance of personal and group responsibilities for an effective discussion. Both scaffold behaviors that are monitored by the teacher in a teacher-guided discussion.

One unique feature of table rounds is the expectation that all participants leave their mark on the community "tablecloth." Part of the set-up for this protocol is the placement of chart or project paper on each table and the provision of a marker or pen to each student. If possible, provide each group of students with a different colored marker so each group's contributions can be identified during the rounds. As the dialogue proceeds, each student jots down thoughts that come to mind on the paper. These can take the form of words or visual representations. Individual contributions are in addition to the summary notes taken by the recorder/reporter. The purpose of this individual writing is twofold; it adds to the body of thinking left behind by each group, and it supports individual focus and accountability.

## FIGURE 6.8

### Student Roles and Responsibilities for Student-Led Dialogue

**Facilitator**
• Poses focus question and asks for a lead-off speaker.
• Keeps group members focused on the question.

**Recorder/Reporter**
• Records main ideas on the "tablecloth."
• Reviews main ideas as the round concludes to verify them with the group.

**Timekeeper**
• Helps facilitator with pacing by alerting the group to time at the midpoint of dialogue.
• Calls time one minute prior to the end of the round to allow the recorder to review big ideas.

**Norms Monitor**
• Reviews the norms with group members at the beginning of the first round.
• Reminds group members of the need to adhere to think time and equitable participation norms.

## FIGURE 6.9

### Norms for Small-Group Discussion

• **Focused Speaking:** Use the focus question to guide thinking and speaking. Stay on topic.

• **Active Listening:** Listen to understand classmates' comments and identify areas of agreement and disagreement.

• **Use of Think Times:** Pause for three to five seconds after a question is asked and following a comment.

• **Equitable Participation:** Monitor your own talking; speak, but don't monopolize. Encourage nonparticipants to contribute.

• **Questioning to Clarify or Expand:** Ask questions when you don't understand another's comment or when you want to hear more about a topic.

• **Piggybacking on One Another's Thinking:** Build on others' ideas to take group thinking deeper.

While students engage in group dialogue, the teacher circulates, listens in for feedback related to deep knowledge, and takes notes. At the end of three rounds, students return to their original stations and engage in final dialogue to identify ways in which visitors to their table added to and took thinking about their question deeper. The teacher may wish to ask for a one-minute report from each table group following this synthesis.

The recommendation is for groups of four. This group size optimizes the opportunity for everyone to contribute to dialogue during each five-minute round. It also allows each student to assume one of the assigned leadership roles. The teacher should create a minimum of three focus questions so each group will have the opportunity to think about three different issues. Of course, the teacher will need to plan rotations in advance to ensure orderly movement of groups during the class.

Like the other group structures related to student-led dialogues, table rounds is for use after surface knowledge has been built. This typically means the structure is most appropriate as a unit draws to a close.

# Featured Protocol: Table Rounds

*(directions for students)*

Today, you are seated with a group that will engage in dialogue over the course of three rounds of discussion. You will think together about three different questions as you move between tables. Your primary purpose is to engage in collaborative dialogue within your group and across groups as you exchange ideas via written notes.

*(directions for teacher)*

1. Organize each group, helping students assign a facilitator, recorder/reporter, timekeeper, and norms monitor. Review the responsibilities associated with each assigned role.

2. Have the norms monitor take a minute to review all six norms and ensure that all group members have a common understanding of them.

3. Tell facilitators to lead the group in a dialogue focused on the question featured at their table. They'll have a total of five minutes to explore the group's thinking about this question.

4. Say, "Timekeepers, your job is to help with pacing and ensure that your group moves along in a timely manner. You should signal the group a minute or so before the allocated time is up to allow closure."

5. During the final minute of each round, make sure the reporters review the big ideas that emerged from the dialogue to ensure they captured the essence of their group's thinking.

6. Say, "Everyone is expected to record insights that come to you on the paper in front of you. You can use words or visual representations to convey your ideas. Those who visit your table next will review your notes and big ideas."

7. Have each group move clockwise to the next table. They should take their markers with them so their group's contributions will stand out from others.

8. After the group has arrived at the new station, the facilitator should read the focus question aloud and pause for a few seconds to afford everyone time to think.

9. The reporter should sit in front of the big ideas recorded by the previous group's reporter. The reporter reads the previous group's big ideas one at a time. As these are read aloud, everyone should be thinking about the extent to which they agree with the ideas and what they might add to them.

10. The facilitator then leads the group in a dialogue on the new question. The reporter takes notes as before. All group members jot down ideas on the space in front of them. Students follow the same steps as before, pausing one minute before the end of their allocated time to let the reporter talk about the big ideas.

11. Have students move once more, following the same protocol.

12. At the end of three rounds, instruct students to return to their original stations. Say, "Your final job is to look at the notes left by the other groups and identify ways in which your classmates have added to and deepened your original thinking about the topic."

## Classroom Artifact

### Roles and Rounds Structure Collaborative Dialogue

Brad Waguespack teaches AP environmental science at Vestavia Hills High School. His students are seniors who come to him with deeply ingrained views of themselves as learners. Brad notes that a perennial challenge is engaging all students in class dialogue. To this end, he has made increased use of collaborative groups. One of his goals is to improve students' ability to self-direct in small-group settings. Designating roles for each group member is a strategy he believes to have advanced this goal. In this video, taken near the end of the school year, students engage in a modified version of table rounds as they review for their AP exam. They assume the following three roles as they participate in this learning activity: questioner, scribe, and facilitator.

### Electronic Options

Student-led feedback can be asynchronous and one-to-one. Flipgrid (https://info.flipgrid.com) is an excellent tool for connecting students for the purpose of providing this type of feedback. Using this technology, students can respond to a teacher prompt via a video recording, upload it to a shared class folder, and give and receive feedback. The teacher can group students so members of a triad, for example, can listen to and provide feedback to one another. The triads might then gather during class for face-to-face interactions to clarify and extend their learning.

Flipgrid is only one example of a technology that can be tapped to enhance student-to-student interactions. Google Docs and a range of Chrome extensions can also be used to support student reflection and exchange thinking prior to face-to-face dialogue. Students almost always benefit from these activities before beginning a class dialogue.

## The End in Mind

Teacher guidance, norms, and protocols help scaffold student thinking and interactions, but the goal is to gradually remove these supports as students build their own capacity to engage in self- and collective regulation. Recall Joseph Roberts, the mathematics teacher at Liberty Middle School, and his students who were featured in the opening video in the introduction. Mr. Roberts reached his goal: to prepare students to interact authentically as they might in real life where they are independent of teacher control and without formal response structures. As these 8th graders neared the end of the year, they were operating as a true community of practice in which they actively regulated their own learning and helped peers increase their understanding. This class exhibited what Carnell (2000) calls "a collaborative learning community where learning is shared and socially constructed." They also engaged in what this researcher calls "co-construction" of knowledge that "is grounded in the assumption that learners are teachers and teachers are learners" (p. 48).

## Feedforward

The skillful use of response structures and quality questions can result in meaningful dialogue that generates feedback nourishing the learning of students and teachers alike. This is dialogic feedback, the focus of the final chapter. Dialogic feedback is a culmination of teacher and students learning new roles, responsibilities, and skills. It occurs when all members of a learning community work together to create a safe environment, when teachers design lessons driven by quality questioning, and when feedback is valued as the ingredient that enhances learning for all.

## Transferring Principles to Practice

Use Figure 6.10 to decide how to use ideas presented in this chapter to plan for and support your students' ability to seek and use formative feedback. Identify practices you are currently using and would like to strengthen as well as others you may wish to consider.

**FIGURE 6.10**

Transferring Principles to Practice: Response Structures

| Opportunities for Practice | Classroom Applications | |
|---|---|---|
| | **Teacher Learning** | **Teacher Facilitation of Student Learning** |
| **Review the criteria for the selection of response structures (Figure 6.1) with members of your collaborative team to make shared meaning.** Talk about why it might be important to determine response structures for use with focus questions as a part of lesson planning and how you might use these criteria in your decision making. | With your collaborative team, dedicate one planning session to the selection of response structures for a given lesson. Think about the focus questions for the lesson and the requirements for each. For each question, brainstorm a list of possible response structures. Use the list of criteria to make decisions about the most appropriate ones. | Conduct a "post-mortem" on the response structures used in a lesson you recently taught. Identify all the response structures used. Using the criteria, reflect on the effectiveness of each. Engage students in this reflection as appropriate. For example, you might ask students to talk about the extent to which identified structures motivate them to respond (accountability) and are relatively easy and comfortable for them to use. |
| **Analyze Figure 6.2 to ensure you understand the organizers: teacher-guided/student-led; surface and deep.** Generate a list of personal insights and questions for sharing with your team members. | Talk with members of your collaborative team about the potential value of Figure 6.2. Think together about the following kinds of questions: *To what extent do we thoughtfully decide when to use a teacher-guided or student-led approach to dialogue? What are the benefits of each? Why is it important to distinguish between response structures appropriate for feedback related to surface and deep knowledge?* | Select one lesson for which you incorporate a teacher-guided dialogue. In advance of this lesson, think about how you can model and scaffold selected skills for students. You may wish to look back at the skills and dispositions featured in Chapter 4 to identify the specific skills you'd like to focus on. Reserve time at the end of the lesson to debrief the experience with your students. |

| Opportunities for Practice | Classroom Applications | |
| --- | --- | --- |
| | Teacher Learning | Teacher Facilitation of Student Learning |
| **Examine the four-step process for use in teacher-guided discussion.** What is your reaction to the suggestion of routinely providing time for individual reflection followed by public sharing prior to the opening of a discussion? What might be the possible benefits? What concerns do you have? | Engage in dialogue with colleagues about the recommended four-step process. Share the ways in which you have previously given students opportunities to review classmates' thinking prior to engagement in a whole-class discussion. Brainstorm other strategies and tools that might be used for this purpose. | Select an upcoming lesson in which you might try out the four-step process. Intentionally design the lesson with the process as the centerpiece. Following the teaching of the lesson, take time to reflect on how it went. Engage students in reflection if appropriate. |
| **Review Figure 6.3 to identify response structures you've used in the past and those you may be interested in trying out.** Reflect on the extent to which you've used a range of structures for both surface and deep/transfer knowledge. | Share your experiences using response structures featured in Figure 6.3 with other members of your team. Talk together about those that have worked most effectively with your students. Identify a structure you and at least one other colleague are willing to try out with your students (one that you've not used previously). Use this structure in a lesson, collect evidence of its effectiveness, and reflect on how it worked. | Use the response structure in the lesson designed with your colleague(s). Collect informal evidence about its effectiveness (e.g., observe and take notes as students engage in responding). Talk with your students about how it worked for them. Organize your evidence in a follow-up dialogue with colleague(s) who used this with their students. |
| **Think about occasions, if any, when you've incorporated student-led dialogue into a lesson.** What structure did you use? What were the positive outcomes? What challenges did they present? | Collectively reflect with team members about past and possible future use of student-led dialogue. Discuss the potential benefits and challenges. Review the protocols included in this chapter to identify one you believe might advance your students' thinking and engagement. Plan to use this during a lesson. | Implement the lesson featuring student-led dialogue. Collect informal evidence about its effectiveness (e.g., observe and take notes as students engage in responding). Talk with your students about how it worked for them. Organize your evidence in a follow-up dialogue with colleague(s) who used this with their students. |

*(continued)*

**FIGURE 6.10—(***continued***)**

Transferring Principles to Practice: Response Structures

| | | |
|---|---|---|
| **Watch the Classroom Artifact video about Joseph Roberts's 8th grade math class.** Reflect on what he might have done to develop his students' capacity to engage in self-directed dialogue (see p. 6). | Watch the video again with members of your team. Engage in collaborative dialogue to identify the specific skills and dispositions exhibited by the 8th graders. Talk about the desirability of developing these with your students—and how you might work together toward this end. | Show this video to students in your class to engage them in reflection focused on their skills and dispositions. Ask them to identify the benefits of students leading their own learning. Ask whether this is a model they would like for their class. (You may want to use a short video clip from one of the videos from elementary classrooms to younger students [K–3] and plan an age-appropriate discussion focused on the same questions.) |

# Part IV

# Advancing Engagement and Learning

The vision for questioning, dialogue, and feedback is to create classrooms in which teachers and students are learning with and from one another. In these classrooms, there is individual accountability and collective responsibility. Students are motivated to take charge of their learning and contribute to a community of learners.

The final chapter revisits the interdependence of questioning, dialogue, and feedback as they interact to produce dialogic feedback. Three primary features of this powerful form of feedback are highlighted: partnership, self-regulation, and social-emotional learning. When these three operate in tandem, they contribute to dialogic feedback and, in turn, are strengthened by intentional use of the principles and practices spotlighted in earlier chapters.

This book is offered as a manual of practice to support educators who believe that "it is right that students are involved in and responsible for their own learning" (Wiliam & Leahy, 2015, p. 129). The featured tools, protocols, and classroom artifacts are a collection from which readers may draw as they chart journeys for themselves and their students. Each journey will be unique, utilizing the strengths of the teacher orchestrators and addressing the interests, needs, and talents of their students. There is no one right pathway, but all who embark share a vision and a common destination: the empowerment of students to engage skillfully and enthusiastically in learning and to self-regulate their own thinking and learning.

# Dialogic Feedback: A Transformative Process

---

*What are the features of dialogic feedback that can transform learning for students and teachers?*

---

Dialogue is the bridge between questioning and feedback. It is the product of two-way communication in which learners compare their current knowledge and skills to a learning goal. Both students and teachers assume the role of learner during these interactions, which include teacher-to-student and student-to-student talk. It also contributes to self-talk, or internal dialogue, for all learners. The feedback borne of this process is *dialogic feedback*, and all who participate become more confident and capable learners. Their motivation or will to learn increases, and they collaboratively create a community that nurtures positive academic and social-emotional outcomes. The 8th grade math students featured in this chapter's first classroom artifact are evidence of what can happen when a teacher commits to the processes featured in this book. This class also illustrates the four themes that are recapped in this final chapter.

- The three constituent processes—questioning, dialogue, and feedback—are interdependent and inseparable.
- Students and teachers work as partners as they engage in the processes.
- Self-regulation is integral to dialogic feedback.
- Social-emotional connections are vital to effective outcomes.

As you finish your reading, you will be invited to self-assess and consider next steps on your personal learning journey.

## Classroom Artifact

### 8th Graders Showcase Benefits of Dialogic Feedback

This video features 8th grade mathematicians at work solving a real-life problem: *How can understanding the rate of soft drink sales at a sporting event enable us to make sound business decisions?* Joseph Roberts created this problem and designed a three-part lesson to build his students' mathematical proficiency while developing important social-emotional skills. In the first part of the lesson, students collaborate to make meaning of a graph depicting the rate of sales over time. They then move to a team consideration of the implications of their findings. Finally, teams share their proposed business plans using data to defend their ideas.

At the beginning of the school year, these students lacked the skills and dispositions required to lead their own learning through questioning and collaborative dialogue. Mr. Roberts was intentional in developing these competencies and in creating classroom experiences that would mimic and prepare his students for real-life learning and work. This video, recorded late in the school year, showcases the benefits that can accrue to students whose teacher commits to these transformative processes.

## Interdependent Processes

Dialogic feedback results from the strategic use of quality questioning, dialogue, and feedback. The quality of the questioning process determines the quality of the dialogue. This, in turn, shapes the nature and quality of the feedback. Figure 7.1 offers a graphic representation of the relationships among these components and the critical qualities of each.

Quality questioning begins with a carefully designed question focused on learning goals and invites students to surface their thinking—not guess the "teacher's answer." Response structures promote responding by all and contribute to an inclusive classroom community. This approach to questioning is necessary to the production of useful dialogue and feedback.

Teacher follow-up questions serve to extend thinking and generate dialogue, initially between the teacher and the responding student. This may lead to student-to-student conversations that can broaden the scope of the resulting feedback. These interactions offer teacher and students alike opportunities to extend their learning through clarification, interpretation, and extension of responses.

**FIGURE 7.1**

Components of Dialogic Feedback

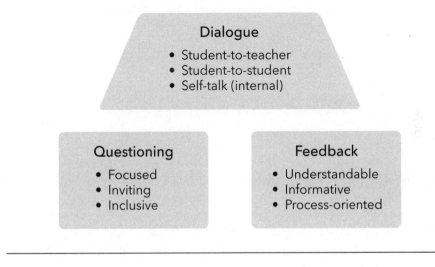

Dialogue makes student thinking visible so the teacher can examine the thinking process each student uses to reach a response. Dialogue also enables everyone to clarify the meaning behind their language so the feedback is understandable. Back-and-forth questions and responses allow all members of the classroom community to make connections to their individual schema so the feedback is informative. Indeed, dialogue is the vehicle by which teachers move from evaluative to interpretive listening in order to scaffold student thinking to a more correct and complete understanding. It is the process by which students compare others' understandings with their own, self-assess, and extend and deepen their knowledge.

Operating together, these three processes can transform learning. They challenge the traditional notion of feedback (i.e., the teacher telling students whether their answer is right or wrong and then providing the right answer), which is ineffective for most students because they lack the skills to translate and act on these statements. As students engage actively through questioning and dialogue, they generate feedback for themselves and their peers. This transformation is fueled by partnerships, contributes to self-regulation, and positively affects social-emotional learning and academic achievement.

---

### Self-Assessment

- To what extent do I understand the connection between quality questioning, dialogue, and feedback?

- In what ways are my beliefs about student learning aligned with the principles underlying this connection?

- What parts of Chapters 1 and 2 would I like to review?

---

## Student–Teacher Partnership

Teachers cannot force students to engage in dialogue or to seek, use, and offer feedback during class conversations. Students must decide the risk is warranted and that their participation will be of value to their learning. They must also understand why the skills and dispositions are important to them as learners. When these conditions are met, students can partner with teachers and one another in learning.

Jim Knight offers a compelling and comprehensive examination of the power of partnership principles in *Unmistakable Impact* (2011). Although Knight applies these principles to professional learning, they also support student learning as it occurs through dialogic feedback. He notes that the partnership approach is guided by this simple idea: "Treat others the way you would like to be treated" (p. 28). He also identifies seven related principles, two of which seem particularly relevant to partnering with students to achieve our results: equality and reciprocity.

### Equality

Knight writes that those who adopt the principle of equality view others as having equal value, thereby listening to everyone with the same care and attention. He notes that "partners do not decide for each other; they decide together" (Knight, 2011, p. 29). Dialogic feedback depends on a teacher–

student relationship imbued with respectful listening and a commitment to exchange information that enables joint decision making about where to go next in learning. A classroom community committed to partnership also supports student-to-student relationships based on mutual trust, respect, caring, and a collaborative approach to learning. Equality is at the center of partnership and dialogic feedback.

## Reciprocity

Knight (2011) defines *reciprocity* as "the belief that each learning interaction is an opportunity for everyone to learn" and is the "inevitable outcome of a true partnership" (pp. 44–45). Indeed, reciprocity is "an integral part of learning, better described as dialogue" (Askew & Lodge, 2000, p. 12). As Brookhart (2017) notes, the most effective feedback involves interaction and "talking when possible" (p. 13).

The reciprocal nature of dialogic feedback stems from the fact that all parties have an expectation for learning. Teachers seek feedback from students through quality questioning practices, and they interpret or translate student responses so they can determine student progress toward established learning goals. This enables teachers to generate and communicate feedback to students. Students, in turn, translate teacher questions or comments into feedback to determine the next steps in their learning.

As a teacher and students seek, provide, and use feedback, they engage in similar processes. Each must *generate* questions and responses to represent their current thinking. They then *communicate* those verbally to make their thinking visible to others. As others respond, they *translate* spoken words to make personal meaning and *integrate* this information into their current understanding. These reciprocal exchanges are visualized in Figure 7.2.

In formative classrooms, students also partner with one another in their learning. Bailey and Heritage (2018) refer to this as coregulation, a socially shared process in which students assume responsibility for giving and receiving feedback from one another as they collaborate to achieve joint learning goals. This involves skills such as turn-taking, use of think times, active listening, and building on others' ideas. Coregulation requires student collaboration, one of the hallmarks of the CORE learning culture presented in Chapter 3. A partnership approach takes root and flourishes in such a culture. Mr. Roberts's 8th graders (featured in the classroom artifact on p. 176) exemplify the essence of coregulation.

**FIGURE 7.2**

Reciprocal Exchanges Associated with Dialogic Feedback

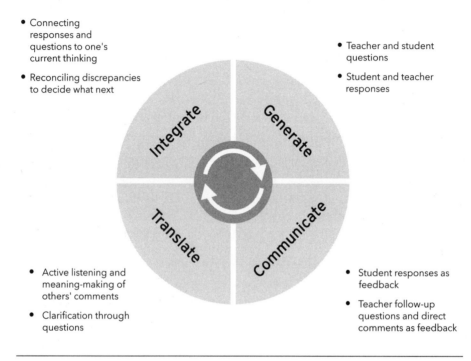

- Connecting responses and questions to one's current thinking
- Reconciling discrepancies to decide what next

- Teacher and student questions
- Student and teacher responses

- Active listening and meaning-making of others' comments
- Clarification through questions

- Student responses as feedback
- Teacher follow-up questions and direct comments as feedback

## Self-Assessment

- What connections do I see between intentional use of partnership principles and dialogic feedback?

- To what extent am I comfortable embracing partnership principles as I work with young people?

- What ideas do I need to continue thinking about as I seek to better understand this shift?

- What parts of Chapters 3 and 4 might I want to review to deepen my understanding of shifting roles and responsibilities?

# Self-Regulation

Effective formative feedback nurtures self-regulated learners. Zimmerman and Schunk (2001) note that "students are self-regulated to the degree that they are metacognitively, motivationally, and behaviorally active participants in their own learning process" (p. 5). Self-regulated learners set individual learning goals, plan how to reach them, monitor their progress, and modify strategies when needed to accomplish their goals. They also develop internal guidance systems that enhance their ability to seek and use feedback and provide feedback to others.

Self-regulated learners approach learning proactively, believing they can learn on their own; they do not simply react to a teacher's instruction. They possess the dispositions presented in Figure 4.8 (p. 102). Key to becoming a self-regulated learner is a willingness to persevere, a desire to work independently, and an ability to imagine new possibilities.

Self-assessment is a core activity for self-regulated learners. The ability to self-assess can be enhanced through practice. When teachers pause during instruction to allow students to seek and use evidence of their progress, students can hone their skills at self-assessment and become more self-regulating. Intentional and consistent use of think times 1 and 2 support self-regulation. These periodic, short timeouts allow students to reflect on and process instruction; therefore, teachers support student self-assessment when they build these pauses into their instruction.

There is a direct connection between the quality of feedback given to students and their ability to self-regulate. External feedback serves as grist for the mill of self-assessment. As students become more proficient in self-assessing, they also become better able to use external feedback (Bailey & Heritage, 2018). The more self-regulated a learner becomes, the more feedback they can be given because they are better able to translate and integrate that feedback into their internal guidance systems.

Ultimately, self-regulation allows students to take charge of their learning in the classroom and beyond. It is an important cornerstone for positive social-emotional well-being, which contributes to learner success.

### Self-Assessment

• To what extent do I understand the relationship between formative feed-back and self-regulation? What questions do I still have?

• How much consideration do I and my colleagues give to student self-regulation? Is this an outcome that we talk about and plan for?

• How might I use the skills presented in Figures 4.3 (p. 97), 4.4 (p. 98), 4.5 (pp. 98-99), and 4.6 (pp. 99-100) and the dispositions outlined in Figure 4.8 (pp. 102-103) to support my students' development of self-regulation?

## Social-Emotional Connections

Effective use of formative feedback depends on both cognitive and emotional factors. Most thought leaders credit formative feedback with increased student engagement and motivation (Brookhart, 2017; Clark, 2012; Duckor & Holmberg, 2017; Shute, 2008; Wiliam, 2011; Yang & Carless, 2013). The process begins when students receive feedback they can use to close gaps in knowledge and skills. As they engage metacognitively to apply feedback, their belief in their ability to learn and achieve increases. This positively influences feelings of self-efficacy (Black & Wiliam, 1998; Shute, 2008), and heightened self-efficacy sustains motivation and engagement. With increased motivation, students are more likely to seek and use additional feedback. Figure 7.3 depicts the cyclical nature of this process and the interdependence of cognitive and social-emotional factors.

The social-emotional climate of a classroom determines the nature and extent of student engagement in these processes. When students feel psychologically safe and comfortable, they are more likely to become actively engaged. Souers and Hall (2019) make a compelling case for creating a "nest" in which students can comfortably learn. This secure learning space is "safe, predictable, and consistent" (p. 23), which is an environment conducive to risk-taking and transparency. Without such an environment, students lack the social and emotional resilience to seek and use feedback.

Souers and Hall (2019) offer what they call the new three Rs: relationship, responsibility, and regulation—components they deem essential to student success. They argue for the infusion of the three Rs into classroom and school environments. Dialogic feedback depends on and strengthens each of these three.

**FIGURE 7.3**

Interdependence of Cognitive and Social-Emotional
Factors in Effective Formative Feedback

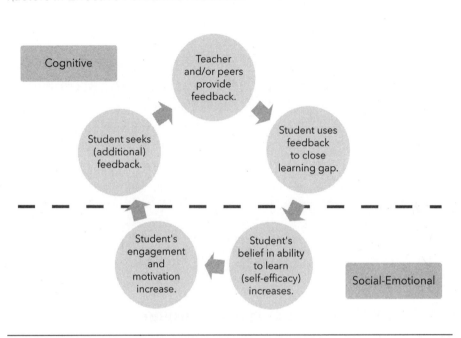

Partnership relationships provide an important cornerstone for social-emotional learning through dialogic feedback. When learners feel their responses are valued, their sense of identity is strengthened. When they engage in reciprocal learning, their self-efficacy is strengthened. This relationship nurtures social and emotional safety. When students are consistently treated with kindness and respect, they become open to relationships based on trust and respect.

Feedback does not become formative until students use it to adjust their learning. This places responsibility on individual learners to seek and utilize feedback related to their learning goals. A formative environment depends on the development of collective responsibility—students' willingness to support one another's learning. The development of student responsibility contributes to their social-emotional well-being, which, in turn, makes them better seekers and users of external feedback.

Self-regulation is a source and product of effective formative feedback. It is also a hallmark of socially and emotionally secure individuals. Development of self-regulatory skills in an academic environment prepares students for self-regulation outside the walls of school.

### Self-Assessment

- What questions do I have about the relationship between effective use of formative feedback and social-emotional learning?

- What concrete steps can I take to create an environment in which students feel safe to seek, use, and generate feedback?

- How can I help my students increase the quality of their relationships with others, the level of their individual and collective responsibility for engaging in dialogic feedback, and the quality of their self-regulatory skills?

## The Vision: Golden Moments in Learning

Recall Hattie and Clark's (2019) idea of a "golden moment in learning when the context is live, the student is 'in the flow,' and the learning is gaining momentum" (p. 82). How many golden moments do you and your students experience in a day, a week, or a year? Whatever the number, each of us wishes for more. Dialogic feedback holds great potential for increasing that number.

Realization of this potential begins with a commitment to partnering with students to develop their capacity to seek, use, and provide feedback as they become more self-regulated. It also requires careful attention to social-emotional factors. Participation in dialogic feedback, in turn, strengthens partnerships, self-regulation, and social-emotional learning.

Working together, these processes transform learning for all. This is the vision: providing students with golden moments in learning that foster success in school and beyond while promoting self-actualization. The hope is that this book will support you in embracing and bringing this vision to fruition.

# Appendix: Classroom Videos

## Summary Listing of Videos

Sprinkled throughout this book are 21 videos of K–12 students and their teachers engaged in learning using the processes featured in *Questioning for Formative Feedback*. Use this QR code to access the entire playlist and hear a brief introduction from the author, Jackie Acree Walsh (http://qrco.de/bcpucF).

| Teacher, Grade Level, and School | Video Title and Description | Location |
|---|---|---|
| Joseph Roberts<br>• 8th grade math<br>• Liberty Middle School, Madison, AL<br><br>http://qrco.de/bcpuea | *The End in Mind: Academic, Social, and Emotional Learning for ALL*<br><br>Students in this 8th grade general math class are collaboratively solving a problem centered on a 2×2 table. They pose questions, respectfully agree and disagree, and reach a shared understanding. Their teacher listens and intervenes only when needed to recenter the conversation. | Introduction, p. 6 |
| Kati Haynes and Heather Pounders<br>• 3rd grade math<br>• Weeden Elementary School, Florence, AL<br><br>http://qrco.de/bcpufo | *Feedback from Students Informs Collaborative Lesson Design*<br><br>Collaborative reflection and planning are routine for these two 3rd grade teachers. In this video, they review three data sources to consolidate feedback regarding individual student progress to plan the next day's learning. They use their conclusions to differentiate the feedback they'll offer various groups of students. | Chapter 1, p. 21 |
| Lory Schieler<br>• 8th grade algebra<br>• Liberty Middle School, Madison, AL<br><br>http://qrco.de/bcpugr | *Ad Hoc Teacher-Led Small Groups: A Forum for Feedback*<br><br>Students build on one another's ideas in a small-group dialogue driven by their teacher's carefully formed questions. Each student identifies the strategy used to solve a given equation, piggybacking on one another's explanations. In the accompanying reflection, the teacher details the techniques she uses to form the ever-changing groups. | Chapter 1, p. 22 |

| Teacher, Grade Level, and School | Video Title and Description | Location |
|---|---|---|
| Anna Wooten<br>• 8th grade ELA<br>• Florence Middle School, Florence, AL<br><br>http://qrco.de/bcpuhj | *Multiple Forms of Feedback Emerge During Literature Circles*<br>Students discuss a novel in small groups where they are challenged to use text-based evidence to support their thinking. The teacher rotates from group to group to pose questions and provide customized feedback. Her end-of-class reflection reveals her rationale for using this response structure to secure feedback from all students. | Chapter 1, p. 30 |
| Samantha Hammond, Jesse Snider, and Anna Wooten<br>• 8th grade ELA<br>• Florence Middle School, Florence, AL<br><br>http://qrco.de/bcpuiD | *Establishing New Norms to Support Thinking and Dialogue*<br>Members of this collaborative team reflect on strategies they used to transform their classrooms from traditional to student-centered learning spaces. The featured norms support new student understandings of the value of wrong answers, think times, and listening and learning from peers. | Chapter 2, p. 46 |
| Mary Busbee<br>• High school biology<br>• Vestavia Hills High School, Vestavia Hills, AL<br><br>http://qrco.de/bcpuis | *Intentional Use of Think Times Transforms Classroom Talk*<br>Students engage in whole-class and small-group dialogue as they explore cell communications. They follow their teacher's lead in using think times to engage in thinking and rehearsing their responses. The result: more elaborated responses and more students actively participating in the class. | Chapter 2, p. 47 |
| Mary Busbee<br>• High school biology<br>• Vestavia Hills High School, Vestavia Hills, AL<br><br>http://qrco.de/bcpujW | *Students Reflect on the Value of Think Times*<br>Five high school students engage in collaborative dialogue as they reflect on the value of think time to their learning. Their comments mirror the findings of researchers and provide powerful testimony to the intentional use of these pauses. | Chapter 2, p. 52 |

| Teacher, Grade Level, and School | Video Title and Description | Location |
|---|---|---|
| Leslie Sedberry<br>• 8th grade ELA<br>• Liberty Middle School, Madison, AL<br><br>http://qrco.de/bcpukH | *Preparing 8th Graders for Whole-Group Discussion*<br><br>Students engage in small-group dialogue in preparation for whole-class discussion of a novel they have been studying. Their use of questioning strategies promotes self-assessment while providing feedback to the teacher on group and individual progress. | Chapter 2, p. 54 |
| Sue Noah, Kate Armstrong, and Anna Underwood<br>• Kindergarten and 1st grade<br>• Athens Elementary School, Athens, AL<br><br>http://qrco.de/bcpukn | *Developing Norms and Procedures with "Littles"*<br><br>Members of this small PLC reflect on the specific tools and strategies they used to support their young students in productive student conversation. They highlight the use of pairs and quads along with the norms they taught and reinforced with their students over the course of a school year. | Chapter 3, p. 66 |
| Jane Haithcock<br>• 8th grade ELA<br>• Liberty Middle School, Madison, AL<br><br>http://qrco.de/bcpulL | *Building a Safe, Comfortable Environment for Reciprocal Feedback*<br><br>Students adopt norms and engage actively in collaborative learning through participation in response structures that support lesson purposes. The teacher's reflection identifies norms and practices she uses to improve and increase feedback to students. | Chapter 3, p. 80 |
| Courtney Evans<br>• 7th grade math<br>• Oxford Middle School, Oxford, AL<br><br>http://qrco.de/bcpum0 | *Three Teacher Roles in Practice*<br><br>Lesson designer, learning facilitator, and culture builder—these three teacher roles are on display as this teacher leads her students from individual to pair to whole-class responding using a range of electronic and traditional response structures. The product of their work is a set of success criteria for a major learning target in their prealgebra curriculum. | Chapter 3, p. 82 |

| Teacher, Grade Level, and School | Video Title and Description | Location |
|---|---|---|
| Samantha Hammond<br>• 8th grade ELA<br>• Florence Middle School, Florence, AL<br><br>http://qrco.de/bcpumw | *Structured Opportunities for Peer Feedback During a Socratic Seminar*<br>Students are paired to serve as feedback partners while engaging in a Socratic seminar. While one partner participates in a conversation in the inside circle, the partners seated in the outside circle observe and take notes—both to provide feedback to their partners based on criteria provided by the teacher and to continue the dialogue in the inner circle. | Chapter 4, p. 89 |
| Lisa Gill and Steven Lavender<br>• 3rd and 4th grade<br>• Athens Elementary School, Athens, AL<br><br>http://qrco.de/bcpunQ | *Strategic Use of Small-Group Structures Scaffolds Social Skills for Young Learners*<br>These teachers use "peanut butter and jelly" partners and "sandwich" groups to structure productive peer dialogue during their math lessons. Students are comfortable providing feedback to one another in these small-group configurations. The teachers circulate and provide targeted feedback to individuals and pairs. | Chapter 4, p. 97 |
| Jessica Sutherland<br>• High school chemistry<br>• Vestavia Hills High School, Vestavia Hills, AL<br><br>http://qrco.de/bcpunq | *Questions to Generate Student-Led Dialogue in a High School Chemistry Class*<br>Students working in structured small groups of three collaboratively discuss quality questions posed by their teacher. The teacher circulates to listen in and coach when needed. She reflects on the extent to which the processes and strategies featured in this book align with those associated with the research-based curricula she uses in her chemistry class. | Chapter 5, p. 115 |
| Steven Lavender<br>• 4th grade math<br>• Athens Elementary School, Athens, AL<br><br>http://qrco.de/bcpuoI | *Activation of Prior Knowledge in a 4th Grade Math Class*<br>Students respond to a question in a quick write as they prepare for an opening discussion designed to surface and assess prior knowledge and skills. The teacher circulates to identify patterns of misunderstanding as he prepares to facilitate the whole-class dialogue. | Chapter 5, p. 117 |

| Teacher, Grade Level, and School | Video Title and Description | Location |
|---|---|---|
| Samantha Hammond, Jesse Snider, and Anna Wooten<br>• 8th grade ELA<br>• Florence Middle School, Florence, AL<br><br>http://qrco.de/bcpuon | *Collaborative Planning of Quality Questions*<br>This three-member ELA team engages in collaborative planning throughout the school year, which is now drawing to a close. They reflect on the value of collaboratively designing quality questions and on how they use students' in-class responses as feedback for their collaborative reflection on how to make future questions more effective. | Chapter 5, p. 124 |
| Sue Noah<br>• Kindergarten<br>• Athens Elementary School, Athens, AL<br><br>http://qrco.de/bcpupE | *A Special Kind of Fishbowl in a Kindergarten Class*<br>First grade students work in pairs as they try out different counting strategies. The teacher circulates, listens in, provides feedback, and identifies student responses worthy of spotlighting. She invites all other students to form a circle around the featured pair who share their strategies. This is a powerful technique for promoting peer feedback with young children. | Chapter 6, p. 147 |
| Jesse Snider<br>• 8th grade ELA<br>• Florence Middle School, Florence, AL<br><br>http://qrco.de/bcpupg | *Integrating Tech Responses into Whole-Class Discussion*<br>In this lesson, students move from using Pear Deck for individual responding to partner dialogue to whole-class discussion. The video includes teacher reflection on the type of feedback emerging from each of these sources and the value of using quality questioning and dialogue to make the thinking behind students' answers visible. | Chapter 6, p. 152 |
| Kate Armstrong<br>• 1st grade math<br>• Athens Elementary School, Athens, AL<br><br>http://qrco.de/bcpuqQ | *Use of Carousel with 1st Graders to Support Dialogic Feedback*<br>First graders in this video work collaboratively to review their understandings of different shapes. Working in groups of four, they rotate to learn from, provide feedback to, and build on previous teams' ideas. | Chapter 6, p. 156 |

| Teacher, Grade Level, and School | Video Title and Description | Location |
|---|---|---|
| Brad Waguespack<br>• Environmental science<br>• Vestavia Hills High School, Vestavia Hills, AL<br><br>http://qrco.de/bcpurH | *Roles and Rounds Structure Collaborative Dialogue*<br><br>In this environmental science lesson, students review for an upcoming AP exam. They participate in collaborative dialogue in response to a question related to a key concept that is formed by one of their members. Over the class period, they rotate through four stations to provide feedback related to previous comments and to add their own thinking. | Chapter 6, p. 168 |
| Joseph Roberts<br>• 8th grade math<br>• Liberty Middle School, Madison, AL<br><br>http://qrco.de/bcpuru | *8th Graders Showcase Benefits of Dialogic Feedback*<br><br>The final video spotlights a student-led dialogue focused on interpretation of a graph depicting soft drink sales at a sporting event. The culminating learning activity challenges teams of students to use their findings and make recommendations that consultants might make to a real-life company providing such a service. | Chapter 7, p. 176 |

# References

Allal, L. (2018). *Self-regulation in learning: The role of language and formative assessment.* Harvard Education Press.

Anderson, L. W., & Krathwohl, D. R. (Eds.). (2001). *A taxonomy for learning, teaching, and assessing: A revision of Bloom's taxonomy of educational objectives.* Addison Wesley Longman.

Askew, S., & Lodge, C. (2000). Gifts, ping-pong, and loops—linking feedback and learning. In S. Askew (Ed.), *Feedback for learning* (pp. 1–18). Routledge.

Bailey, A. L., & Heritage, M. (2018). *Self-regulation in learning: The role of language and formative assessment.* Harvard University Press.

Black, P., Harrison, C., Lee, C., Marshall, B., & Wiliam, D. (2003). *Assessment for learning: Putting it into practice.* Open University Press.

Black, P., & Wiliam, D. (1998). Inside the black box: Raising standards through classroom assessment. *Phi Delta Kappan, 80*(2), 139–144.

Black, P., & William, D. (2009). Developing the theory of formative assessment. *Educational Assessment, Evaluation and Accountability, 21,* 5–31.

Bransford, J. D., Brown, A. L., & Cocking, R. R. (Eds). (2000). *How people learn: Brain, mind, experience, and school.* Committee on Developments of Science in Learning and Committee on Learning Research and Educational Practice. National Academies Press.

Brookhart, S. (2001). Successful students' formative and summative use of assessment information. *Assessment in Education, 8*(2), 153–169.

Brookhart, S. (2017). *How to give effective feedback to your students* (2nd ed.). ASCD.

Butler, D., & Winne, P. (1995). Feedback and self-regulated learning: A theoretical synthesis. *Review of Educational Research, 65*(3), 245–281.

Byrnes, J. P. (2007). *Cognitive development and learning in instructional contexts* (3rd ed.). Pearson.

Carless, D. (2013). Trust and its role in facilitating dialogic feedback. In D. Boud & L. Molloy, (Eds.), *Effective feedback in higher and professional education* (pp. 90–103). Routledge.

Carless, D., & Boud, D. (2018). The development of student feedback literacy: Enabling uptake of feedback. *Assessment & Evaluation in Higher Education, 43*(8), 1315–1325.

Carnell, E. (2000). Dialogue, discussion, and feedback—view of secondary school students on how others help in their learning. In S. Askew (Ed.), *Feedback for Learning* (pp. 46–62). Routledge.

Carver, S. M. (2006). Assessing for deep understanding. In S. K. Sawyer (Ed.), *The Cambridge handbook of the learning sciences* (pp. 205–224). Cambridge University Press.

City, E. A., Elmore, R. F., Fiorman, S. E., & Tietel, L. (2009). *Instructional rounds in education: A network approach to improving teaching and learning.* Harvard Education Press.

Clark, I. (2012). Formative assessment: Assessment is for self-regulated learning. *Educational Psychology Review, 24,* 205–249.

Clark, I. (2014). Equitable learning outcomes: Supporting economically and culturally disadvantaged students in formative learning environments. *Improving Schools, 17*(1), 116–126.

Clarke, S. (2000). Getting it right—distance marking as accessible and effective feedback in the primary classroom. In S. Askew (Ed.), *Feedback for learning* (pp. 32–45). Routledge.

Conley, D. T. (2008). *College knowledge: What it really takes for students to succeed and what we can do to get them ready.* Jossey-Bass.

Costa, A. L., & Kallick, B. (2014). *Dispositions: Reframing teaching and learning.* Corwin.

Daggett, W. (2012). *The Daggett system for effective instruction: Alignment with student achievement.* International Center for Leadership in Education.

Danielson, C. (2013). *The framework for teaching evaluation instrument, 2013 edition.* The Danielson Group.

Dillon, J. T. (1988). *Questioning and teaching: A manual of practice.* Teachers College Press.

Duckor, B., & Holmberg, C. (2017). *Mastering formative assessment moves: 7 high-leverage practices to advance student learning.* ASCD.

DuFour, R., & Eaker, R. (1998). *Professional learning communities at work: Best practices for enhancing student achievement.* Solution Tree.

Fredricks, J. A. (2014). *Eight myths of student engagement: Creating classrooms of deep learning.* Corwin.

Frey, N., Hattie, J., & Fisher, D. (2018). *Developing assessment-capable visible learners, grades K–12.* Corwin.

Furtak, E. M., Glasser, H. M., & Wolfe, Z. M. (2016). *The feedback loop: Using formative assessment data for science teaching and learning.* NSTA.

Hargreaves, E. (2005). Assessment for learning? Thinking outside the (black) box. *Cambridge Journal of Education, 35*(2), 213–224.

Hargreaves, E., McCallum, B., & Gipps, C. (2000). Teacher feedback strategies in primary classrooms—new evidence. In S. Askew (Ed.), *Feedback for learning.* Routledge.

Hattie, J. (2008). *Visible learning: A synthesis of over 800 meta-analyses relating to achievement.* Routledge.

Hattie, J. (2012). *Visible learning for teachers: Maximizing impact on learning.* Routledge.

Hattie, J., & Clarke, S. (2019). *Visible learning feedback.* New York: Routledge.

Hattie, J., & Donoghue, G. (2016). Learning strategies: A synthesis and conceptual model. *NPJ Science of Learning 1,* 16013.

Hattie, J., & Timperley, H. (2007). The power of feedback. *Review of Educational Research, 77*(1), 81–112.

Hattie, J., & Zierer, K. (2017). *10 mindframes for visible learning: Teaching for success.* Routledge.

Jiang, Y. (2014). Exploring teacher questioning as a formative assessment strategy. *RELC Journal, 45*(3), 287–304.

Juzwik, M. M., Borsheim-Black C., Caughlan, S., & Heintz, A. (2013). *Inspiring dialogue: Talking to learning the English classroom.* Teachers College Press.

Knight, J. (2011). *Unmistakable impact: A partnership approach for dramatically improving instruction.* Corwin.

Love, N., Smith, N., Whitacre, R., & Haley-Speca, M. (2020). *Coaching high-impact teacher teams: Four steps to improving student achievement.* Research for Better Teaching.

Marzano, R. J. (2017). *The new art and science of teaching.* Solution Tree.

Marzano, R. J., & Simms, J. A. (2014). *Questioning sequences in the classroom.* Marzano Research Laboratory.

Mazur, E. (2013). *Peer Instruction: A user's manual.* Pearson.

Mehan, H. (1979). *Learning lessons: Social organization in the classroom.* Harvard University Press.

Michener, C. J., & Ford-Connors, E. (2013). Research in discussion: Effective support for literacy, content, and academic achievement. In J. Ippolito, J. Lawrence, & C. Zaller (Eds.), *Adolescent literacy in the era of the common core: From research into practice* (pp. 85–102). Harvard Education Press.

National Academies of Sciences, Engineering, and Medicine. (2018). *How people learn II: Learners, contexts, and cultures.* National Academies Press.

National Council for the Social Studies. (2013). *The college, career, and civic life (C3) framework for social studies state standards: Guidance for enhancing the rigor of K–12 civics, economics, geography, and history.* Author.

National Governors Association Center for Best Practices, Council of Chief State School Officers. (2010). *Common core state standards.* Author.

NGSS Lead States. (2013). *Next generation science standards: For states, by states.* National Academies Press.

Nicol, D. (2010). From monologue to dialogue: Improving written feedback in mass higher education. *Assessment and Evaluation in Higher Education, (31)*1, 501–517.

Nicol, D., & Macfarlane-Dick, D. (2006). Formative assessment and self-regulated learning: A model and seven principles of good feedback practice. *Studies in Higher Education,* 31(2), 199–218.

Oczkus, L. D. (2018). *Reciprocal teaching at work: Powerful strategies and lessons for improving reading comprehension* (3rd ed.). ASCD.

Organization for Economic Co-Operation and Development. (2005 November). Formative assessment: Improving learning in secondary classrooms. *Policy Brief.* OECD Washington Center.

Palincsar, A. S., & Ladewski, B. G. (2006). Literacy and the learning sciences. In R. K. Sawyer (Ed.), *The Cambridge handbook of the learning sciences* (pp. 299–316). Cambridge University Press.

Ritchhart, R., Church, M., & Morrison, K. (2011). *Making thinking visible: How to promote engagement, understanding, and independence for all learners.* Jossey-Bass.

Rowe, M. B. (1974). Wait times and rewards as instructional variables, their influence in language, logic, and fate control: Part one—wait time. *Journal of Research in Science Teaching, 11*(2), 81–94.

Rowe, M. B. (1986, January–February). Wait time: Slowing down may be a way of speeding up! *Journal of Teacher Education, 37*(1), 43–50.

Sadler, D. R. (1989). Formative assessment and the design of instructional systems. *Instructional Science, 18,* 119–144.

Sadler, D. R. (2010). Beyond feedback: Developing student capacity in complex appraisal. *Assessment and Evaluation in Higher Education, 35*(5), 535–550.

Sawyer, R. K. (2006). *The Cambridge handbook of the learning sciences.* Cambridge University Press.

Schlechty, P. C. (2011). *Engaging students: The next level of working on the work.* Jossey-Bass.

Schmoker, M. (2011). *Focus: Elevating the essentials to radically improve student learning.* ASCD.

Shute, V. J. (2008). Focus on formative feedback. *Review of Educational Research, 78*(1), 153–189.

Souers, K. V., & Hall, P. (2019). *Relationship, responsibility, and regulation: Trauma-invested practices for fostering resilient learning.* ASCD.

Sutton, P. (2009). Towards dialogic feedback. *Critical and Reflective Practice in Education, 1*(1), 1–10.

Tobin, K. (1986). Effects of teacher wait time on discourse characteristics in mathematics and language arts classes. *American Educational Research Journal, 2392,* 191–200.

Vygotsky, L. S. (1978). *Mind and society: The development of higher psychological processes,* 14th ed. The President and Fellows of Harvard College.

Wagner, T. (2010). *The global achievement gap: Why even our best schools don't teach the new survival skills our children need—and what we can do about it.* Basic Books.

Walsh, J. A. (2021). *Empowering students as questioners: Skills, strategies, and structures to realize the potential of every learner.* Corwin.

Walsh, J. A. (2016). *Improving classroom discussion* (Quick Reference Guide). ASCD.

Walsh, J. A., & Sattes, B. D. (2005). *Quality questioning: Research-based practice to engage every learner.* Corwin.

Walsh, J. A., & Sattes, B. D. (2015). *Questioning for classroom discussion: Purposeful speaking, engaged listening, deep thinking.* ASCD.

Walsh, J. A., & Sattes, B. D. (2016). *Quality questioning: Research-based practice to engage every learner* (2nd edition). Corwin.

Wiggins, G. (2012). 7 keys to effective feedback. *Educational Leadership, 70*(1), 10–16.

Wiliam, D. (2011). *Embedded formative assessment.* Solution Tree.

Wiliam, D. (2018). *Embedded formative assessment* (2nd edition). Solution Tree.

Wiliam, D., & Leahy, S. (2015). *Embedding formative assessment: Practical techniques for K–12 classrooms.* Learning Sciences International.

Willingham, D. (2009). *Why don't students like school? A cognitive scientist answers questions about how the mind works and what it means for the classroom.* Jossey-Bass.

Winne, P. H., & Butler, D. L. (1994). Student cognition in learning from teaching. In T. Husen & T. N. Postlethwaite (Eds.), *International encyclopedia of education* (2nd ed., pp. 5738–5745). Pergamon.

Yang, M., & Carless, D. (2013). The feedback triangle and the enhancement of dialogic feedback processes. *Teaching in Higher Education, 18*(3), 285–297.

Zimmerman, B. J., & Schunk, D. H. (Eds.). (2001). *Self-regulated learning and academic achievement: Theoretical perspectives* (2nd ed.). Routledge.

# Index

The letter *f* following a page number denotes a figure.

# About the Author

**Jackie Acree Walsh,** PhD, is a consultant and author who dedicates significant time to working with teachers and school leaders to embed quality questioning into their daily practice. To this end, she has facilitated professional learning across the United States, authored seven books and multiple articles on the topic, and made frequent presentations at professional conferences. Walsh began her career as a high school social studies teacher and has worked and taught at all levels of education. Her passion is partnering with educators to improve learning for all students. A lifelong learner, she is an avid reader, traveler, and conversationalist. She is also a sports enthusiast with a special interest in teams representing her alma maters, Duke University and the University of Alabama. Her greatest joy comes from time shared with her children and grandchildren. Contact Walsh at walshja@aol.com and follow her on Twitter @Question2Think.

## Related ASCD Resources: Formative Feedback

At the time of publication, the following resources were available (ASCD stock numbers in parentheses).

*Advancing Formative Assessment in Every Classroom: A Guide for Instructional Leaders, 2nd Edition* by Connie M. Moss and Susan M. Brookhart (#120005)

*Better Learning Through Structured Teaching: A Framework for the Gradual Release of Responsibility, 3rd Edition* by Douglas Fisher and Nancy Frey (#121031)

*Cultivating Curiosity in K–12 Classrooms: How to Promote and Sustain Deep Learning* by Wendy L. Ostroff (#116001)

*Fast and Effective Assessment: How to Reduce Your Workload and Improve Student Learning* by Glen Pearsall (#118002)

*The Formative Assessment Action Plan: Practical Steps to More Successful Teaching and Learning* by Nancy Frey and Douglas Fisher (#111013)

*The Formative Assessment Learning Cycle* (Quick Reference Guide) by Susan M. Brookhart and Jay McTighe (#QRG117085)

*Generating Formative Feedback* (Quick Reference Guide) by Jackie Acree Walsh (#QRG122060)

*How to Give Effective Feedback to Your Students, 2nd Edition* by Susan M. Brookhart (#116066)

*Improving Classroom Discussion* (Quick Reference Guide) by Jackie Acree Walsh (#QRG117053)

*Now That's a Good Question! How to Promote Cognitive Rigor Through Classroom Questioning* by Erik M. Francis (#116004)

*Questioning for Classroom Discussion: Purposeful Speaking, Engaged Listening, Deep Thinking* by Jackie Acree Walsh and Beth Dankert Sattes (#115012)

*Questioning Strategies to Activate Student Thinking* (Quick Reference Guide) by Jackie Acree Walsh (#QRG117054)

For up-to-date information about ASCD resources, go to www.ascd.org. You can search the complete archives of *Educational Leadership* at www.ascd.org/el.

### ASCD myTeachSource®

Download resources from a professional learning platform with hundreds of research-based best practices and tools for your classroom at http://myteachsource.ascd.org/

For more information, send an email to member@ascd.org; call 1-800-933-2723 or 703-578-9600; send a fax to 703-575-5400; or write to Information Services, ASCD, 1703 N. Beauregard St., Alexandria, VA 22311-1714 USA.

# WHOLE CHILD
# **TENETS**

## **HEALTHY**

Each student enters school healthy and learns about and practices a healthy lifestyle.

## **SAFE**

Each student learns in an environment that is physically and emotionally **safe** for students and adults.

## **ENGAGED**

Each student is actively engaged in learning and is connected to the school and broader community.

## **SUPPORTED**

Each student has access to personalized learning and is supported by qualified, caring adults.

## **CHALLENGED**

Each student is challenged academically and prepared for success in college or further study and for employment and participation in a global environment.

# THE WHOLE CHILD

The ASCD Whole Child approach is an effort to transition from a focus on narrowly defined academic achievement to one that promotes the long-term development and success of all children. Through this approach, ASCD supports educators, families, community members, and policymakers as they move from a vision about educating the whole child to sustainable, collaborative actions.

*Questioning for Formative Feedback* relates to the **challenged, engaged,** and **supported** tenets. *For more about the ASCD Whole Child approach, visit* **www.ascd.org/wholechild.**